TWO PLAYS

T0347778

Ödön von Horváth

TWO PLAYS

DON JUAN COMES BACK FROM THE WAR
Translated by Christopher Hampton

FIGARO GETS DIVORCED
Translated by Ian Huish

OBERON BOOKS
LONDON

WWW.OBERONBOOKS.COM

First published in these translations in 1991 by Absolute Classics
Reprinted in this volume by Oberon Books Ltd
(incorporating Absolute Classics)
521 Caledonian Road, London N7 9RH
Tel: +44 (0) 20 7607 3637 / Fax: +44 (0) 20 7607 3629
e-mail: info@oberonbooks.com
www.oberonbooks.com

PB ISBN: 9780948230394
E ISBN: 9781783197880

Cover design: Konstantinos Vasdekis

Visit www.oberonbooks.com to read more about all our books
and to buy them. You will also find features, author interviews and
news of any author events, and you can sign up for e-newsletters
so that you're always first to hear about our new releases.

Contents

5

Introduction

The two plays in this volume were both written in the late 1930s when their author was already an exile from Hitler's Third Reich. They are less overtly linked to the political events of the late twenties and early thirties than his earlier, better-known plays, yet their themes are political in a much broader sense than the *Volksstücke*, of which *Tales from the Vienna Woods* is the most acclaimed and most widely performed. These later plays reflect the problems of inflation, displacement and exile that have an uncanny topicality for Europe in these last decades of the twentieth century.

Horváth was born in 1901 in Fiume, today Rijeka in Yugoslavia, describing himself as a 'typical old Austro-Hungarian mixture: Magyar, Croatian, German, Czech: my name is Magyar, my mother tongue German.' In an age and a country where racial purity was at such a premium Horváth prided himself in interviews on the heterogeneous branches of his own family tree. He regarded himself as an outsider in Germany, looking at events and people as an observer, 'a faithful chronicler of my time'. This was above all true of the plays he wrote between 1927 and 1932, notably *Sladek the Black Militia Man, Italian Night, Tales from the Vienna Woods, Kasimir and Karoline* and *Faith Hope and Charity*. In all of these he portrays a society in decay with all its latent – and not so latent – brutality, racism and mean-mindedness. The characters in them, especially the men, are eagerly waiting to hail the institutionalized violence of a state run by Fascism. There is much talk in *Sladek* of nationalism of a peculiarly repulsive kind, and uniforms in varying shades of black and brown feature prominently. In *Tales from the Vienna Woods* knives are brandished ominously; in *Italian Night* rifles are both seen and heard; the ironically titled *Faith Hope and Charity* shows a sinister and heartless bureaucracy backed up by an inquisitorial police machine. This last play went into rehearsal just before the *Machtergreifung* of 1933 but was not performed in Germany until after the war.

In the years after 1933 the emphasis in Horváth's writing shifted away from social criticism to centre on the individual and his conscience. In the last year of his life Horváth changed to the novel form, producing in quick succession two brilliant first-person narrations that examine such problems, through the eyes of a teacher, in *Youth Without God*, and a soldier, in *A Child of Our Time* (a work whose title Michael Tippett borrowed for his oratorio). When he was killed in a freak accident during a thunderstorm on the Champs Elysées on 1 June 1938 Ödön von Horváth was already working on a third such novel. Its title was to be *Adieu Europa* and its narrator a writer, contemplating his own social role and political responsibility. The last words of the short fragment that Horváth had completed stand as an epitaph to the thirty-six-year-old writer and are a fitting comment on his own exile:

Why was it that I had to leave my home? What did I stand up for? I never took part in politics. I stood up for the rights of the human being. But perhaps my crime was that I found no solution.

I go on writing my feuilleton and I don't know the answer. I don't know it yet. The sea roars. New waves and still more new waves keep on coming. Again and again and again.

There is evidence that Horváth had begun work on a Don Juan play as early as 1934; there also exists among his papers a film synopsis, intriguing in its similarities to and differences from the play, called *A Don Juan of Our Time*. In his treatment of the story Horváth reverses the traditional role of Don Juan as seducer of women and makes him their victim. To judge from the accounts we have of his own powerful effect on women, the appeal of the theme for Horváth is hardly surprising: what is interesting is his decision, writing at a catastrophic moment in German history, to set the play at a time of earlier catastrophe, when post-war optimism and good intentions were nipped ferociously in the bud. The play's bleakness and drained pessimism show that Horváth writing a historical play on a classical theme, had lost nothing of his prophetic power. His colleague, Franz Theodor Csokor, writing to a mutual friend, described the play as 'perhaps his most mature work to date.'

The play was first performed at the Theater der Courage in Vienna on 12 November 1952 under the title *Don Juan Comes Back*: at that date it was thought that any reference to the war in the title of a play might be tactless.

Figaro Gets Divorced is ostensibly lighter in mood than *Don Juan Comes Back from the War* and it is tempting to see this as a deliberate reflection of Mozart's operas on the same subjects, where this is certainly the case. However the darkness of the opening scene – 'It is a pitch black night' – is also the darkness Horváth mentions in his preface to the play: 'Humanity is only a weak light in the darkness.' The play is set in the thirties and deals with the plight of people in exile, people exiled both from their country and their social status. The Count Almaviva simply does not understand that the world has changed and that his rank now means nothing: Figaro on the other hand adapts with alarming facility, cutting his coat according to the new cloth with no problems until Susanne makes him realise that he has lost his humanity in the process. The consequences of such fickleness and such willingness to oblige one's new masters are revealed as being not only hollow but dangerous. It is fitting that this version of *Figaro Gets Divorced* received its premiere in this country in the very year that more than one Count returned to the land of revolution in Eastern Europe to reclaim his castle; when more than a few pillars of the tumbled communist regimes fitted in to the new structures with remarkable ideological flexibility.

The translations both follow the texts published in Horváth's *Collected Works* by Suhrkamp Verlag in 1972. In the case of *Figaro Gets Divorced* material from both the original thirteen-scene version and from the shortened nine-scene Prague version has been used.

Christopher Hampton,
Ian Huish, 1991

DON JUAN COMES BACK FROM THE WAR

I should like, once again, to thank Ian Huish and
Maximilian Schell for their help in checking the translation.

CH

Preface

W e do not know whether Don Juan ever had a historical
existence. All that can be established is that there was
once a Don Juan type, and consequently it is clear that there
still is and always will be. I have, therefore, felt free to describe
a Don Juan of our time, since our own times are always more
immediate to us. Of course, this Don Juan, too, ostensibly
belongs to the past, as he died during the great inflation of
1919–23 in other words at a time when, even in the most banal
sense of the word, all values were dislocated. However, as I
say, this time is only ostensibly in the past, because from a
somewhat broader point of view, we are still living in times of
inflation, and there is no telling when they will end.

A typical feature of our age is the way each individual
changes radically as a result of the catastrophes which befall
society as a whole. Thus Don Juan comes back from the war
and imagines he has become a different man. Nevertheless he
remains who he is. He has no choice. He is not going to escape
the ladies.

For hundreds of years, people have tried to solve the enigma
of Don Juan in a variety of ways, but the enigma is insoluble.
The character has gone through the most disparate
transformations, from the original view of him as adulterer,
murderer and desecrator of the dead to the psychologically
dissected weary cavalier. He lives on in tradition and legend
as a violent criminal, like some force of nature, running riot
against morality and justice. He is the great seducer, seduced
again and again by women. They all succumb to him, but –
and this may be the essential point – he is never really loved
by any of them. (This is why the play does not have a single
love scene.)

So what is it that attracts women to Don Juan? It is not
male sexuality alone, although no doubt he is its most powerful
representative, but the particularly ardent and exclusively
distinct metaphysical implications of this sexuality, which give

him such inescapable power over women. Don Juan is forever in search of perfection, in other words something which does not exist in the world. And time and again women want to prove to him, and also to themselves, that it is possible for him to find in the world everything he is searching for. The misfortune of these women is that their horizons are worldly – only when they suspect, to their horror, that he is not searching for life but yearning for death, do they recoil from him. Don Juan's tragic guilt is that he continually forgets or even mocks this yearning, and thus becomes the cynical victim of his own powers, but not unaffectingly.

Ödön von Horváth

Characters

DON JUAN

THIRTY-FIVE WOMEN

These thirty-five women not only can but must be played by far fewer actresses, so that almost every actress has several parts to play. I make this observation not only with an eye to the practicability of this play, but prompted by something that has long been established: namely, that there are not thirty-five different types of women, but significantly fewer. The same basic types recur again and again and should be played on the stage by the same women. It was, nevertheless, very necessary to portray thirty-five women, in order to illustrate how the individual basic types can develop. And now a correct dramatis personae, in order of appearance:

DON JUAN

TWO AGEING SOUBRETTES

THREE WOMEN

GRANDMOTHER

MAID

TWO GIRLS OF EASY VIRTUE

MATRON

NURSE

WIDOW

TWO DESIGNERS

WAITRESS

MOTHER

HER TWO DAUGHTERS

FOUR LADIES

LADY FROM BERNE

FAT WOMAN

BLONDE

BRUNETTE

NEIGHBOUR

MASKED LADY

TWO OLD WOMEN

TWO VILLAGE GIRLS

LANDLADY

TWO LITTLE GIRLS

And now a list of the distribution of the individual women's parts, bearing in mind their basic type (with the acts in which they appear in brackets):

FIRST PART: First Ageing Soubrette (I), Matron (I, II), Mother (II, III), First Old Woman (III).
SECOND PART: Second Ageing Soubrette (I), Widow (II), First Lady (II, III).
THIRD PART: First Woman (I), Neighbour (II), Second Old Woman (III), Landlady (III).
FOURTH PART: Grandmother (I, III).
FIFTH PART: Maid (I, III), Second Lady (II, III), Masked Lady (III).
SIXTH PART: First Girl of Easy Virtue (I), Waitress (II), Third Lady (II).
SEVENTH PART: Second Girl of Easy Virtue (I), Second Daughter (II, III), First Village Girl (III).
EIGHTH PART: Nurse (I), First Designer (II), First Daughter (II, III), Fourth Lady (II).
NINTH PART: Second Designer (II), Lady from Berne (II).

The Second Village Girl may be added either to the sixth or the ninth part.

The remaining parts are very small. They are:
Second and Third Women (I), Fat Woman (II), Blonde (II), Brunette (II), First and Second Little Girls (III).

ACT ONE

The War is Over
1. Theatre at the front
2. Street
3. The Grandmother's room
4. Street corner
5. The Second Girl's room
6. Hospital
7. The Grandmother's room

ACT TWO

The Chaos of Inflation
1. Hospital
2. Café
3. The Mother's spare room
4. A Profiteer's house
5. Box at the Opera House
6. At the ice-rink
7. The Mother's spare room
8. The Designers' Studio
9. The Mother's spare room

ACT THREE

The Snowman
1. Stairwell
2. The Mother's spare room
3. The Profiteer's house
4. The forest deep in snow
5. The Snowman
6. Room at the inn
7. In front of the Grandmother's house
8. Cemetery

Don Juan Comes Back from the War was first performed in this translation at the National Theatre (Cottesloe) on 18 April 1978, with the following cast:

DON JUAN, Daniel Massey

THE WOMEN, Polly Adams, Sheraton Blount, Judi Bowker, Edna Doré, Susan Fleetwood, Irene Gorst, Susan Littler, Louisa Livingstone, Elspeth March, Helen Ryan, Tel Stevens and Janet Whiteside

Director, Stuart Trotter

Designer, Tanya McCallin

Time and Place

The play begins in the late autumn of 1918 and covers a relatively short time-span. It has three acts and twenty-four scenes. Naturally, these are not scenes in the strict sense of the word, but almost always small sketches which happen in the smallest possible space. The settings need only be indicated, not simply to enable the individual acts to be played without a break, but also to do justice to the language.

ACT ONE: The War is Over

Theatre at the Front

Late autumn, 1918. A theatre in a barracks at the front. Extremely primitive dressing-room. Two SOUBRETTES, already somewhat long in the tooth, are packing their trunks. Away in the distance, a drum-roll and a trumpet-call. It's raining.

FIRST SOUBRETTE: The war's over. We lost.

SECOND SOUBRETTE: I can't find my red wig.

FIRST SOUBRETTE: The director's back at headquarters. The reserves have mutinied and that fat colonel's been cashiered. There aren't any more officers. The general's a sergeant.

SECOND SOUBRETTE: Wish I'd never signed that bloody contract. Playing a soubrette at the front, I gave my Ophelia here once, you know. Do you think there'll be a show this evening?

FIRST SOUBRETTE: God knows. Main thing is, peace is on the way.

SECOND SOUBRETTE: All I want to know is, are conditions going to improve in the theatre...there's my red wig. (*She puts it on like a hat; an alarm-clock goes off.*) Shut up!

(*The SECOND SOUBRETTE switches it off.*)

FIRST SOUBRETTE: (*Looking at the clock.*) It's a historic day, today. At twelve o'clock the armistice starts.

SECOND SOUBRETTE: (*In front of the mirror.*) Another twenty minutes, then.

(*Away in the distance, a grenade explodes.*)

FIRST SOUBRETTE: I wonder how many more are going to die...

SECOND SOUBRETTE: It's the women I feel sorry for, the ones without a man.

FIRST SOUBRETTE: The things you say. Men are human beings as well, aren't they?

SECOND SOUBRETTE: No.
(*DON JUAN enters; he's wearing a filthy uniform, no decorations, unarmed.*)
FIRST SOUBRETTE: (*Confused.*) What do you want?
DON JUAN: (*To the SECOND SOUBRETTE.*) I'm looking for you. We know each other.
SECOND SOUBRETTE: Do we? I can't say I...
DON JUAN: I saw you in two operettas.
SECOND SOUBRETTE: (*Suddenly interested.*) Which ones?
DON JUAN: (*Gazing at her.*) I can't remember the names. All I know is, you were standing down by the prompter's box and waiting. You knew he was coming. White curtains, do you remember? That was the first one. Then you were writing a letter, it was at night and you knew he'd answer. That was the other one. The way you smile reminded me of a woman I knew before the war, a hundred years ago, I sometimes think. Mm. Will you accept a small gift, to thank you for reminding me... (*He smiles and hands her a small packet.*) Cigarettes, the spoils of war. They're genuine Egyptian... (*He bows to the SECOND SOUBRETTE and exits.*)
SECOND SOUBRETTE: Well, what about that then?
FIRST SOUBRETTE: Mad.

Back Home

WOMEN queue in front of an empty grocer's shop.

FIRST WOMAN: No bread, no salt, no lard...is this supposed to be peace?
SECOND WOMAN: Don't take on, the main thing is our men are back from those mass graves at the front.
FIRST WOMAN: Well, my husband never even heard the guns, I wish he had, but he's got flat feet and he was stuck at home for the duration, and I only have to open my mouth to get clouted...so, war or peace, it's all the same to me.
THIRD WOMAN: It's wrong to talk like that. My poor Josef is stuck in Siberia somewhere, and who knows

when he'll be back. You'll only know how much you miss the beatings, when there's no one there to beat you any more.

FIRST WOMAN: I don't give a damn about men!

(*DON JUAN appears and approaches the WOMEN.*)

DON JUAN: I'm looking for the caretaker's wife...

FIRST WOMAN: (*Confidently interrupting him.*) That's me.

DON JUAN: Your husband told me you'd be here, I've just been to see him...

FIRST WOMAN: (*Interrupting him again.*) What do you want?

DON JUAN: Just some information. (*He looks around, as if he were being followed; slowly.*) It was before the war, there was a young lady, lived in your building, third floor on the left...that's who I'm looking for. Your husband told me she'd moved, but he couldn't remember where to...

FIRST WOMAN: (*Gazing at him.*) A lady... (*She starts suddenly and recognises DON JUAN, frightened.*) Jesus, Mary and Joseph, now I know who you are! God save us, I thought you were dead.

DON JUAN: (*Smiles gently.*) I was on the missing list.

FIRST WOMAN: Well, miracles never cease. Yes, the young lady, she's gone. She lives with her grandmother.

DON JUAN: (*Pricks up his ears, surprised.*) Where's that?

FIRST WOMAN: Oh, what's it called, that place? (*She looks it up in her notebook.*) There we are, that's it.

(*She shows DON JUAN the address. He reads it.*)

DON JUAN: Long way away.

WOMAN: Yes.

(*Silence.*)

DON JUAN: (*Slowly.*) When did she leave?

FIRST WOMAN: Nineteen-fifteen. I remember the exact day, it was the day of our great victory at Gorlice. There was a storm, our flag got all ripped.

DON JUAN: I was at Gorlice.

FIRST WOMAN: Oh, yes? Well, it's all in the past, isn't it? (*Silence.*)

DON JUAN: So that's why she never answered me, I wrote to her, six weeks ago it must have been...

21

FIRST WOMAN: We always forward everything, but there's a lot of post goes astray when there's a war on.

DON JUAN: Yes. (*He looks upwards.*) Who lives there now, third floor on the left?

FIRST WOMAN: A lady dentist. Everything's changed since before the war. All the dentists were killed and the women did the training. Personally, I wouldn't go to one myself, I wouldn't have the confidence.

DON JUAN: (*Again smiles gently.*) Why ever not? (*He looks round again, as if he were being followed.*) Well, I'll be on my way then. To see her grandmother. (*Exits.*)

FIRST WOMAN: Bon voyage, sir, bon voyage! (*She turns quickly to the other WOMEN.*) Do you know who that was? He was famous all over the town for his scandalous love-affairs. He deserted his fiancée just before the wedding, just before the war, and got up to all sorts, knocked around with hundreds of good-for-nothing girls; and his fiancée was pure as the driven, a proper angel. And now, it seems, he's regretting it…Well, if that Don Juan'd been my fiancé I'd've strangled him!

THIRD WOMAN: (*Maliciously.*) And I suppose you didn't give a damn about him, either?

FIRST WOMAN: (*Grinning.*) That's another story.

Small Town

The GRANDMOTHER sits there in her easy-chair, reading the latest newspaper.

GRANDMOTHER: (*Shouting.*) Anna! Anna!
(*The MAID appears.*)
It says in the paper, the armistice was yesterday, and now the looting's started, here as well. They've killed the butcher and wounded the timber-merchant. Shut the windows, shut the doors, come on, I want them double-locked, you silly goose!

MAID: (*Letting fly at her.*) I'm not a silly goose, is that understood? It's a new era now, here as well, and maids are going to have to be treated differently as well, is that understood?

GRANDMOTHER: (*Shrieking.*) It may be a new era for you, but I'm going to say what I like. I'm seventy-six years old and I've seen it all, war and peace and revolutions...so I'm not going to change! Now I want everything locked and bolted!

MAID: (*Sarcastically.*) Double-locked, oh, yes!

(*The MAID exits.*
The GRANDMOTHER looks after her, furious.)

GRANDMOTHER: (*Mumbling.*) Pig.

(*The doorbell rings.*
The GRANDMOTHER jumps and listens fearfully, then shrieks out again.)

Anna! Anna! Who's at the door, who's there?

(*The MAID enters with a letter.*)

MAID: (*With some solemnity.*) It's a letter...

GRANDMOTHER: A letter? Who'd be writing to me?

MAID: It's not for you, it's for Fräulein...

GRANDMOTHER: Who?

(*The GRANDMOTHER gets up, frightened.*)

MAID: It's for your poor granddaughter.

(*Silence.*)

GRANDMOTHER: Show me.

MAID: (*Giving her the letter.*) It's come from the front.

(*The GRANDMOTHER stares at the envelope, considering.*)

Poor thing, she's been dead two years and now she gets a letter...

GRANDMOTHER: (*Interrupting her.*) Send it back.

MAID: Who to, the war?

(*The GRANDMOTHER makes a sudden decision and tears open the letter and reads.*)

GRANDMOTHER: 'Dearest'...oh, it's him, is it... (*She skims through it.*) 'I'm on my way and I'm yours alone'... (*She looks up.*) Yours alone? She's dead. (*She crosses herself.*) God help him...

Street Corner

Night. The moon lights up a sign, which says: 'Anyone passing this point will be shot!' Barbed wire. TWO GIRLS OF EASY VIRTUE appear. The FIRST GIRL suddenly pulls the SECOND GIRL back.

FIRST GIRL: (*Muted.*) Stop! Can't you read?

SECOND GIRL: (*Noticing the sign.*) Oops-a-daisy.

FIRST GIRL: One more step and they shoot to kill. It's the reds over there.

SECOND GIRL: I had a white yesterday.

FIRST GIRL: Sky-blue-pink, what's the difference?... (*She glances apathetically at a poster on the wall in the moonlight.*) Wives, mothers, daughters. Where are your men? In the mass graves. An end to male domination... (*She turns away and grins.*) An end to it.

(*DON JUAN appears and is passing.*)

SECOND GIRL: (*Muted.*) Stop!

(*DON JUAN stops.*)

Anyone passing this point will be shot!

DON JUAN: Why's that?

FIRST GIRL: (*To the SECOND GIRL.*) I like him. He wants to know why he's going to be shot... (*To DON JUAN.*) Are you a foreigner?

DON JUAN: (*Smiles.*) No. I come from the moon.

SECOND GIRL: Tell us something about the moon.

DON JUAN: Everything on the moon is dead... (*He notices the sign and the barbed wire for the first time.*) How do I get to the station?

FIRST GIRL: The station's a pile of smoking ruins. It got bombed. Don't you read the papers?

DON JUAN: No.

FIRST GIRL: Where are you going, then?

DON JUAN: Home.

SECOND GIRL: To your mother?

DON JUAN: (*Looks up.*) That'd be nice.

FIRST GIRL: There are no trains. All the wheels have fallen still, by the power of your will. Are you red or white?

DON JUAN: I'm nothing at all. (*He looks through his timetable.*) I have to change once more, once, that's all. I could be there by now.

(*Gunfire in the distance.*)

SECOND GIRL: Shooting again.

DON JUAN: That was a light machine-gun. Where can I spend the night here?

FIRST GIRL: With us. The hotels are full of soldiers.

(*Silence.*)

DON JUAN: I just want somewhere to sleep, nothing else.

FIRST GIRL: Is that all? We have a price-list.

DON JUAN: (*Smiles.*) I'm not in the market.

(*Silence.*)

FIRST GIRL: Then I'd rather stay where I am.

SECOND GIRL: (*To the FIRST GIRL.*) You'll get shot.

FIRST GIRL: There's always drunks.

SECOND GIRL: (*To DON JUAN.*) Come on.

The Second Girl's Room

Bare room with a bed, a sofa and an iron washstand. DON JUAN enters with the SECOND GIRL. She turns the light on.

SECOND GIRL: Welcome to the château.

DON JUAN: I'll sleep on the sofa.

SECOND GIRL: Sleep in the bed if you like...

DON JUAN: No thanks. (*He looks round, as if he were being followed.*) It smells of lilac.

SECOND GIRL: You're joking.

DON JUAN: But it really does smell of lilac. Is it late?

SECOND GIRL: No, it's far too early.

(*DON JUAN sits on the sofa.*)

DON JUAN: Could you open the window, please?

SECOND GIRL: The window? You want it to get colder?

DON JUAN: I'm hot.

SECOND GIRL: (*Looking at him.*) Have you got a temperature? Watch out, there's some mysterious epidemic going round, people are dying like flies.

Everything's infected, the air's full of germs. They're
calling it flu, but it's the plague. Are you worn out?

DON JUAN: Yes.

SECOND GIRL: (*Pointing to her heart.*) Pains there?

DON JUAN: Yes.

SECOND GIRL: Come on, get into bed, I'll cover you up.

DON JUAN: (*Tired smile.*) You're a nice girl.

SECOND GIRL: I'm only nice because I like you. Go on,
lie down.

DON JUAN: (*Gets up.*) No, I mustn't catch anything. (*Paces
up and down.*)

SECOND GIRL: (*Hurt, ironic.*) Saving up for something
better?

DON JUAN: If you like.
    (*Silence.*)

SECOND GIRL: Are you married?

DON JUAN: (*Smiles gently.*) Nearly.

SECOND GIRL: Engaged then?

DON JUAN: I'm faithful.

SECOND GIRL: (*Smiles.*) Since when?

DON JUAN: Since the war...
    (*Slight grin. The SECOND GIRL stares at DON JUAN
    suddenly.*)

SECOND GIRL: Pity.

DON JUAN: Quiet! (*He listens.*) Somebody called out my
name just now. (*He looks upwards.*)

SECOND GIRL: What is your name?

DON JUAN: Who lives upstairs?

SECOND GIRL: There's just the roof up there, that's all.

DON JUAN: Really?

SECOND GIRL: Yes.
    (*DON JUAN lies down on the sofa.
    The SECOND GIRL sits on the bed and watches him.*)
    Were you in the war long?

DON JUAN: As long as it lasted.

SECOND GIRL: On the Eastern front?

DON JUAN: Everywhere.
    (*Silence.*)

SECOND GIRL: My father was killed at Gorlice.

DON JUAN: I was at Gorlice.

SECOND GIRL: Perhaps you knew my father? He was with the hundred and twenty-fourth regiment, exceptionally tall man with a black beard...

DON JUAN: Didn't know him.

SECOND GIRL: Pity.

(*The SECOND GIRL smiles gently and lies down. Silence.*)

DON JUAN: Who's that under the bed?

SECOND GIRL: (*Up quickly, frightened.*) What? Where?

(*She has a look, nervously.*) There's nothing there...

DON JUAN: Looked like a big dog.

SECOND GIRL: I think you really have got a temperature, you're hallucinating...

DON JUAN: (*Getting up again.*) I'm not ill, I just feel so wretched...

SECOND GIRL: Better lie down then.

DON JUAN: No. (*He paces up and down.*) Have you any writing paper?

SECOND GIRL: (*Confused.*) Why?

DON JUAN: Because I want to write a letter...

SECOND GIRL: (*Grins.*) To your fiancée?

DON JUAN: Yes. Perhaps you are right, perhaps I'm ill, and it's going to take a bit of time... (*He clutches at his heart and sits down again on the sofa.*) I really wanted to surprise her.

SECOND GIRL: Is it a long time since you've seen her?

DON JUAN: Not since before the war.

SECOND GIRL: (*Ironic.*) And you think she's been faithful?

DON JUAN: (*Hesitates; then, with certainty.*) Yes.

SECOND GIRL: (*Ironic.*) I suppose she wrote to you every day?

DON JUAN: No. Never. Quite rightly. It was my fault we separated...but she's waiting for me.

SECOND GIRL: You sound very sure of that...

DON JUAN: I know it.

(*DON JUAN lies down again. Silence.*)

SECOND GIRL: I've never met anyone like you. But perhaps I've never known a real man, because they'd all gone off to the war, by the time I started.

DON JUAN: When was that?

SECOND GIRL: I've forgotten... (*Grins.*)

DON JUAN: I haven't.

SECOND GIRL: All I know is, it was raining. There's your writing paper. (*She puts it on the table.*)

DON JUAN: (*Faintly.*) Thanks.

(*Silence.*)

SECOND GIRL: Where does your fiancée live?

DON JUAN: With her grandmother.

(*The SECOND GIRL yawns, undresses mechanically.*)

SECOND GIRL: Men, you don't deserve women... My God, compared to my poor father, what are you? Nothing. Just nothing. (*She yawns again.*) Fit for the scrap-heap. I hate you all, I really do... Are you listening?

(*DON JUAN has lost consciousness.*)

Hey. Hey!...What's the matter? (*She crosses slowly to the sofa, bends over and looks at DON JUAN.*) Are you dead, or what?

Hospital

The YOUNG NURSE is on duty in the hospital. Night. The MATRON comes in on her rounds.

MATRON: Any developments?

NURSE: That man we'd given up for lost, matron, he's come to.

MATRON: Has he?

NURSE: Only for a few minutes, but the MO thinks he's out of danger.

MATRON: Do we know who he is yet?

NURSE: Only that he's come back from the war, and the MO thinks, judging by his scars, that he must have been seriously wounded... (*She looks around, anxiously.*) He's possessed with evil, matron.

MATRON: What are you talking about?

NURSE: He started talking to his fiancée, saying he was
sorry for everything... Real mortal sins, he was talking
about, terrible, I've never heard anything like it, but
while he was describing them, he was proud of them, it
was like he was boasting...

MATRON: His temperature's a hundred and...

NURSE: (*Interrupting her.*) No, it wasn't just his temperature,
it's all true, everything he said. I'm sure it is... He's the
Devil, Matron!

MATRON: Be quiet!

(*Silence.*)

NURSE: I've nursed him up to now, but I don't want to
nurse him any more.

(*Silence.*)

MATRON: It's your duty to nurse the Devil himself, if he's
ill. (*She starts to leave, then turns back to the NURSE.*)
There's only One Person you can turn to, if you want to
get away from yourself, you know that.

(*The NURSE starts and gazes at the MATRON.*)

Peace be with you.

(*The MATRON exits.*)

The Grandmother's Room

*Back in the small town. The GRANDMOTHER sits in her easy-chair,
reading a letter. The MAID is scrubbing the floor.*

GRANDMOTHER: He's still sick, otherwise he'd be here
already. He says he was badly wounded, and that's when
he knew for the first time, you should only belong to one
person. Yes, I know, he got frightened of going to Hell,
and decided to put everything right.

(*The GRANDMOTHER sniggers grimly.*)

MAID: Shouldn't you write and tell him the poor thing's
been dead for ages?

GRANDMOTHER: You get on with the floor!

MAID: After all, it's the fifth letter...

GRANDMOTHER: He can go on writing till the Devil comes for him! (*She looks at the letter again and grins.*) He says he's searching for his soul!

MAID: (*Suddenly letting fly at her.*) Why don't you leave the dead in peace!

(*Silence.*)

GRANDMOTHER: You know what he did to her, you know the way she died...just let him look for her now. I want to tell him myself, it was him that killed her. All I want is to live long enough to see him come here and...

MAID: (*Interrupting her.*) He won't come if he doesn't get an answer.

GRANDMOTHER: He'll come.

MAID: Never.

(*Silence.*)

GRANDMOTHER: (*Beadily.*) How do you know? You don't even know him.

MAID: No. But I can imagine him.

GRANDMOTHER: (*Sarcastically.*) What's he look like, then?

MAID: That's not the point. He could be a hunchback.

(*Silence.*)

GRANDMOTHER: Hunchback or not, he's going to be standing here in front of me, you'll see, even if I have to wait a hundred years, I'll wait, because I want to wait...

(*The doorbell rings.*

The GRANDMOTHER jumps.

The MAID exits, to open the door.

The GRANDMOTHER listens fearfully, then shrieks out.)

Anna! Anna! Who's at the door, who's there?

MAID: (*Entering.*) Just a beggar.

GRANDMOTHER: You didn't give him anything, did you?

MAID: No.

(*The MAID starts scrubbing the floor again.*

The GRANDMOTHER reads the paper.)

GRANDMOTHER: Your 'new era' didn't last long, then, did it? Beggars are still beggars. It says in the paper the old times are on the way back...

MAID: (*Muttering.*) Not for you...
GRANDMOTHER: (*Looking up.*) Did you say something?
MAID: No. Nothing.

End of Act One.

ACT TWO: The Chaos of Inflation

Hospital

Two months later. A corridor in the hospital. The MATRON is explaining to a heavily-veiled WIDOW the sudden death of her husband.

WIDOW: I can't seem to grasp it.

MATRON: The Lord giveth and the Lord taketh away.

WIDOW: Four years he was in the trenches and only two slight wounds, but now, when it's peace at last, he dies in bed, of a cold...

MATRON: The flu epidemic is part of the war as well, you know.

WIDOW: (*Sobbing.*) My husband, oh, my husband! (*She pulls herself together.*) Aren't I allowed to see him?

MATRON: Give us ten minutes, my dear. We're just dressing him.

(The MATRON nods to the WIDOW, friendly, and starts to exit, left.

DON JUAN enters from the left. He is collarless, unshaven and looks yellow and tired.)

DON JUAN: (*To the MATRON.*) Has the post arrived, Matron?

(Hearing DON JUAN's voice, the WIDOW looks up.)

MATRON: (*To DON JUAN.*) Yes.

DON JUAN: Nothing for me again?

MATRON: (*Staring at him.*) Tell me: what is it you've been waiting for for eight weeks?

DON JUAN: An answer. But if I don't get one...

MATRON: (*Interrupting him.*) Then what?

DON JUAN: (*Grinning.*) Then nothing. It's all water under the bridge.

(*Silence.*)

MATRON: You ought to find yourself a hobby...

(The MATRON exits, left. DON JUAN watches her go.)

DON JUAN: A hobby?

(*DON JUAN smiles gently and passes the WIDOW on his way out, right. The WIDOW suddenly grabs his arm. DON JUAN stops, confused.*)

What do you want?

WIDOW: (*Slowly.*) It is you, isn't it?

DON JUAN: (*Uncomprehending.*) Who? Who am I supposed to be? (*He looks around, as if for help.*)

WIDOW: We know each other.

DON JUAN: Oh. I can't really tell through the veil...

(*DON JUAN smiles. The WIDOW lifts the veil. She's an old woman. DON JUAN shrinks back from her, embarrassed.*)

To be honest, I...

WIDOW: (*Interrupting him.*) How's your fiancée?

(*DON JUAN starts and looks at her.*)

Is she happy with you? Or has she deceived you as much as you deceived me? Is she faithful to you? After all, she is an angel, isn't that right?

(*The WIDOW laughs.*)

DON JUAN: Now I know who you are...

WIDOW: (*Viciously.*) Recognised me, have you?

DON JUAN: The way you laughed . . .

(*DON JUAN clutches at his heart and buckles slightly. The WIDOW watches him.*)

WIDOW: (*Maliciously.*) Pains there?

DON JUAN: (*Tired smile.*) My heart's not been quite right since the war...the flu's made it worse...

WIDOW: (*Slowly, beadily.*) You had it as well, then, the flu?

DON JUAN: Quite badly.

WIDOW: And you're still alive.

DON JUAN: I think so...

(*DON JUAN grins.*
Silence.)

WIDOW: My husband died.

DON JUAN: I'm very sorry...

WIDOW: (*Interrupting him.*) Shut your mouth. (*Silence.*) He forgave me everything, my husband, me and you. Now he's dead and you're alive. You... (*She lets fly at DON JUAN.*) Why aren't you dead and buried? What is it you

33

want from people? You just bring bad luck, wherever you turn up, nothing but bad luck.

(*Silence.*)

DON JUAN: (*Slowly.*) I think I've been transformed by the war...

WIDOW: (*Sarcastically.*) With your talent?

DON JUAN: I think I've lost that.

WIDOW: No. You're just the same.

DON JUAN: I'm tired of it.

WIDOW: You ought to be exterminated.

DON JUAN: I know I'm no good for women.

(*DON JUAN smiles, gently.*)

WIDOW: You won't escape them.

Café

Two (Women) DESIGNERS are sitting in a side-room in a small café in a city. The sun is shining outside, but the curtains are thick. The orchestra is playing a Boston. There's dancing in the main room.

FIRST DESIGNER: There's a man I could go for.

SECOND DESIGNER: Where?

FIRST DESIGNER: Something about him.

SECOND DESIGNER: I can't see him from here.

FIRST DESIGNER: Go over and have a look.

SECOND DESIGNER: You want me to go over? Because of a man? Oh, Peter, whatever next?

FIRST DESIGNER: He can't find a seat.

SECOND DESIGNER Aren't we being a bit silly?

FIRST DESIGNER: Here he is!

(*DON JUAN appears, followed by the WAITRESS, who is helping him out of his coat.*)

DON JUAN: Isn't there a café somewhere without an orchestra?

WAITRESS: No.

DON JUAN: Is there dancing everywhere?

WAITRESS: It's been years since we've had dancing, now we're making up for it.

DON JUAN: Even at lunchtime?

WAITRESS: Even first thing in the morning.

DON JUAN: Mm. (*He sits down.*) Cognac.

(*The WAITRESS exits. DON JUAN starts writing a letter.*)

SECOND DESIGNER: (*To the FIRST DESIGNER, who is still ogling DON JUAN.*) Shall we dance?

FIRST DESIGNER: I'm going to dance with him...

SECOND DESIGNER: Are you out of your mind?

FIRST DESIGNER: (*Getting up.*) I'm going to ask him...

SECOND DESIGNER: If you do that...

FIRST DESIGNER: (*Interrupting her.*) Don't threaten me, Charlie! (*She goes over to DON JUAN.*) May I ask...

DON JUAN: (*Uncomprehending.*) What?

FIRST DESIGNER: I'd like to dance with you.

DON JUAN: (*Confused.*) Dance?

FIRST DESIGNER: It may surprise you, a woman asking you to dance, but the world's changed, you know, why should all the Don Juans be men? What are you writing?

DON JUAN: A letter.

FIRST DESIGNER: Business letter?

DON JUAN: (*Smiles.*) Yes.

FIRST DESIGNER: Let me see your handwriting...

DON JUAN: Why?

FIRST DESIGNER: I know a bit about these things.

DON JUAN: Will the envelope do?

FIRST DESIGNER: Sure. (*She looks at the envelope, her eyes widen; murmurs.*) Good God...

(*DON JUAN considers the FIRST DESIGNER.*)

DON JUAN: (*Suddenly.*) So, you want to dance with me?

FIRST DESIGNER: (*Gazing at him.*) Yes.

DON JUAN: (*Smiles.*) I'm afraid, I've forgotten how to...

FIRST DESIGNER: (*Automatically.*) You can't have.

DON JUAN: (*Staring at her.*) And I don't know anything about these new dances...

(*DON JUAN gets up.*)

FIRST DESIGNER: (*Quite subdued.*) You just have to walk it. Come on, I'll lead...

(*The FIRST DESIGNER exits with him into the main room. The SECOND DESIGNER is alone. She watches them go,*

*then gets up, crosses to DON JUAN's table and reads the
letter he's started.)*

SECOND DESIGNER: 'I've cried out to you, but there's
been no reply... All right, then, I'll stay the man I am.'
(She looks over at the main room.) And who's that?
*(The WAITRESS appears with the cognac.
The SECOND DESIGNER doesn't see her coming.)*

WAITRESS: Is that your letter?

SECOND DESIGNER: *(Startled.)* No.
*(The SECOND DESIGNER puts the letter down on the
table quickly and smiles, embarrassed.)*

WAITRESS: Back where you came from! Move!

SECOND DESIGNER: Don't you speak to me like that!

WAITRESS: Move! Otherwise I'll tell your friend about
that proposition you made me, you walking
catastrophe...
*(The WAITRESS puts the cognac down on DON JUAN's
table and exits.
The SECOND DESIGNER goes back to her place, buries
her face in her hands and weeps.
DON JUAN comes back from the dance-floor with the FIRST
DESIGNER, but they don't sit down.)*

DON JUAN: So you're a designer?

FIRST DESIGNER: Yes. *(She shows him a small scarf.)* Stuff
like this, that's what I do. *(She sticks it in his top pocket.)*
Batik. It's my own design.

DON JUAN: Thanks.

FIRST DESIGNER: And I'm learning to draw.

DON JUAN: Really?

FIRST DESIGNER: I'd like to draw you sometime.

DON JUAN: What good would that do you?

FIRST DESIGNER: I've never drawn a man before.

DON JUAN: Just landscapes, you mean?

FIRST DESIGNER: No. Just women.
(Pause.)

DON JUAN: Do you want to dance?

FIRST DESIGNER: *(Softly.)* Yes.

DON JUAN: But only till it starts getting dark...

(*DON JUAN smiles.*)

FIRST DESIGNER: (*Confused.*) What do you mean by that?

DON JUAN: I've been ill for eight weeks and as today's the first mild day we've had, I've been allowed out of hospital, but I have to go back soon so I don't have a relapse, a relapse would be dangerous. It's my heart... (*DON JUAN smiles.*)

FIRST DESIGNER: What's wrong with you?

DON JUAN: Fairly bad flu, I've had.

FIRST DESIGNER: (*Anxiously.*) You're not still infectious, are you?

DON JUAN: (*Smiles.*) No, I'm harmless now...

FIRST DESIGNER: Because I don't want to die just yet.

DON JUAN: Neither do I... (*DON JUAN stares at her suddenly.*)

FIRST DESIGNER: (*Uncertainly.*) What's the matter?

DON JUAN: You, my dear, you remind me. Of someone who hasn't given me an answer...

FIRST DESIGNER: (*Gazing at him.*) Since when have I been your dear?

DON JUAN: (*Ignoring her question.*) In fact you don't look at all like her... (*DON JUAN clutches at his heart. Pause.*)

FIRST DESIGNER: (*Suddenly.*) Come on... (*The FIRST DESIGNER exits with DON JUAN into the main room. The SECOND DESIGNER, alone, suddenly shouts out.*)

SECOND DESIGNER: The bill! The bill! (*The WAITRESS appears.*)

WAITRESS: I'm not deaf. That's three million. (*The SECOND DESIGNER pays and stands up. Grins.*) Looks as if your friend's been seduced...

SECOND DESIGNER: (*Dully.*) Do you know that man? (*The WAITRESS looks over towards the main room.*) Who is he?

WAITRESS: He does look familiar, somehow...

The Mother's Spare Room

The widow of a professor, a victim of the inflation, has to let out one of her two rooms. She is the MOTHER of Two DAUGHTERS: the FIRST, a twenty-year-old office worker, the SECOND, a fifteen-year-old, who hangs around the house. At the moment, the MOTHER is rummaging through a drawer, while the SECOND DAUGHTER is standing in front of the wardrobe mirror.

SECOND DAUGHTER: Have you pawned the candlesticks?

MOTHER: Yes.

SECOND DAUGHTER: That's the lot, then.
 (*The SECOND DAUGHTER looks at her legs in the mirror.*)

MOTHER: We still have seventeen billion. (*She grins and then suddenly looks serious; dully.*) I could always hang myself.

SECOND DAUGHTER: I wish you wouldn't keep moaning, Mama! What d'you expect me to say about it? At least you've had a good time, you've been to the Riviera and Paris and Norway, what about me? All I've ever heard, for as long as I can remember, is you moaning on, it's enough to make you curl up and die!

MOTHER: Are you blaming me?

SECOND DAUGHTER: Of course I'm blaming you, it's your fault, nobody else's! Why didn't you let me study last year, when our money was still worth something? I could be on stage by now and we wouldn't have to let your room, but a dancer for a daughter wasn't grand enough for you, was it? Not like pawning everything, that's much grander, isn't it, Frau Professor? Well, I'll tell you this: I'm not going to stay here and rot with you, Frau Professor...

MOTHER: Gretl, Gretl, you're so vicious...

SECOND DAUGHTER: Papa would have let me be a dancer. Papa was a practical man.

MOTHER: (*Flaring up.*) What do you know about your father? You weren't even ten when he went off to the war.

SECOND DAUGHTER: Shut up you! I read the letters he
sent you from the front...

MOTHER: (*Interrupting her.*) What?

SECOND DAUGHTER: That's right. Yesterday. I had
nothing else to do, so I broke into your desk, Frau
Professor...

MOTHER: You ought to be ashamed of yourself.

SECOND DAUGHTER: You're the one who ought to be
ashamed! You know what Papa said in his letters, and
you also know why you didn't let me read them. What
was it they said, Frau Professor?

MOTHER: (*Shouting.*) Don't keep calling me Frau
Professor!

SECOND DAUGHTER: (*Shouting her down.*) Let Gretl
learn what she wants to, that's what Papa said, the times
are changing!

(*Silence. The MOTHER suddenly flies at the SECOND
DAUGHTER.*)

MOTHER: Will you stop looking at your legs!

SECOND DAUGHTER: (*Contemptuously.*) Why shouldn't
I? If you've got good legs, you might as well show them
off...

MOTHER: My husband, oh, my husband...look down from
Heaven!

(*The bell rings.*)

SECOND DAUGHTER: That'll be the coalman.

MOTHER: Tell him to come back tomorrow.

(*The MOTHER's about to go and answer the door.*)

SECOND DAUGHTER: (*Sarcastically.*) I suppose you'll be
able to pay him tomorrow?

MOTHER: You be careful God doesn't punish you.

(*The MOTHER exits.*
*The SECOND DAUGHTER watches her go, shrugs her
shoulders, hums a Boston and dances.*
The MOTHER re-enters, this time with DON JUAN.
*The SECOND DAUGHTER, surprised, breaks off in the
middle her dance and looks at him.*
DON JUAN has been watching her dance. He smiles.)

(*To the SECOND DAUGHTER.*) This gentleman wants to rent the room, the Matron told him I was thinking of letting it. (*To DON JUAN.*) This is my daughter.
(*DON JUAN gives a slight bow.*)
And this is the room. It backs on to the garden, it's very quiet.
(*DON JUAN looks round.*)
You'll have everything you need.
(*DON JUAN looks at the SECOND DAUGHTER's legs.*)

DON JUAN: Yes.

MOTHER: Won't you sit down?

DON JUAN: Thank you.
(*DON JUAN sits at the table with the MOTHER.*
The SECOND DAUGHTER sits down a little way off and watches DON JUAN rather shyly.)
I like the room. I'll take it.

MOTHER: The rent is...

DON JUAN: (*Interrupting her.*) Makes no difference.

SECOND DAUGHTER: (*Dully.*) Wonderful.

MOTHER: (*To the SECOND DAUGHTER.*) Gretl... (*She turns, smiling, to DON JUAN.*) Might I ask what your profession is, sir?

DON JUAN: (*Smiles.*) It's a question I ask myself every so often. Before the war, I didn't need to work, but during the war I seem to have lost all my money...and now, well, now I'm an art-dealer.
(*The SECOND DAUGHTER pricks up her ears.*)

MOTHER: Ah.

DON JUAN: Yes. A short time ago, by some absurd fluke, I came into contact with some people who work in design. You know, batik, ceramics, graphics, woodcuts even. A girl I know, a designer, persuaded me to organise the selling of that kind of thing. It won't buy you a castle, what you make out of it, but anyway, it's a living, people want to get rid of their money before it's entirely worthless, so you hardly need to be a born salesman. Yesterday, for instance, I sold a stamp collection... Ludicrous, isn't it? You could call me a racketeer, if you like, a hyena of the inflation.

(*DON JUAN smiles.*)
MOTHER: Oh no, you're not a hyena, not you...
DON JUAN: Let's hope not.
(*The FIRST DAUGHTER arrives back from the office.*)
MOTHER: (*To DON JUAN.*) My elder daughter...
(*DON JUAN stands up.*)
(*To the FIRST DAUGHTER.*) Our lodger.
FIRST DAUGHTER: (*To DON JUAN.*) You don't have to
get up. (*To the MOTHER.*) I have to go in a minute.
MOTHER: Where to?
FIRST DAUGHTER: You know very well, Mama!
MOTHER: Not the Party again?
FIRST DAUGHTER: For ever and ever.
MOTHER: (*To DON JUAN; ironically.*) My daughter wants to
improve the world...
FIRST DAUGHTER: (*Grins.*) Got it in one.
DON JUAN: (*Smiles.*) My respects.
FIRST DAUGHTER: (*Annoyed.*) Thanks. (*To the MOTHER.*)
I'd just like something to eat, quickly.
MOTHER: There's nothing there.
FIRST DAUGHTER: But I left some of my lunch specially.
SECOND DAUGHTER: (*Cheekily.*) I polished that off for
you.
FIRST DAUGHTER: What, again?
MOTHER: Please, I don't suppose our visitor is very
interested...
FIRST DAUGHTER: (*Interrupting her.*) It's quite possible
our visitor isn't very interested in whether people get
enough to eat or not...
MOTHER: Magda! The things you say lately...
FIRST DAUGHTER: (*Interrupting her.*) The things I say are
the right things, believe me!
MOTHER: (*To DON JUAN.*) She's a fanatic... (*To the FIRST
DAUGHTER.*) Do your duty at the office, be honest,
work hard, stay loyal and what more do you need?
FIRST DAUGHTER: (*Flaring up.*) Don't talk rubbish,
Mama! You don't even know what an office looks like,
you've never had to work. Papa always looked after you

and you never gave it a thought. Who was to blame for the war, then? Your world!

DON JUAN: (*Smiles.*) There'll always be wars, Fraulein...

FIRST DAUGHTER: You think so?

DON JUAN: Yes.

MOTHER: Of course there will.

(*Silence.*)

FIRST DAUGHTER: (*To DON JUAN.*) Were you in the war?

DON JUAN: Yes.

FIRST DAUGHTER: (*Sarcastically.*) At HQ?

DON JUAN: (*Staring at her.*) No. In fact I was seriously wounded, but the dear old war had its good side as well. (*He smiles cynically.*) Take me, for example: because of the war I became a better person, and only now it's peacetime I'm beginning to get back to my old self again...

(*The MOTHER laughs.*

The SECOND DAUGHTER contemplates her legs.

The FIRST DAUGHTER gazes at DON JUAN.)

FIRST DAUGHTER: I can't understand it, a man who thinks like that, what's the point of living?

MOTHER: (*Letting fly at the FIRST DAUGHTER.*) Magda! For goodness' sake have some consideration!

DON JUAN: (*To the MOTHER.*) Excuse me! (*To the FIRST DAUGHTER.*) The point of my living, you'll have to ask God that.

FIRST DAUGHTER: All God is is an illusion to console the exploited masses with the idea of a hereafter.

DON JUAN: God, how pathetic...

(*DON JUAN grins.*

The First Daughter is thrown.)

FIRST DAUGHTER: Why are you staring at me like that?

DON JUAN: You've got spirit.

FIRST DAUGHTER: (*Furious.*) Huh!

(*The FIRST DAUGHTER exits quickly.*)

MOTHER: (*To DON JUAN.*) She's mad. Ideals, that's all it is...

DON JUAN: It'll pass.

SECOND DAUGHTER: (*To DON JUAN.*) Why aren't you in films?

DON JUAN: (*Perplexed.*) In films? Me?

SECOND DAUGHTER: Your profile's so good.

MOTHER: (*Sighing.*) Now she's starting. (*To DON JUAN.*) Complete nonsense!

DON JUAN: Why? Films have a future, no doubt about it.

SECOND DAUGHTER: (*To the MOTHER.*) Hear that? That's absolutely killing!

(*The SECOND DAUGHTER laughs. DON JUAN gazes at her. She stops laughing suddenly.*)

DON JUAN: (*To the MOTHER.*) Strange. The way your daughter just said 'absolutely killing' suddenly reminded me of someone...

SECOND DAUGHTER: Asta Nielsen, I bet.

DON JUAN: No, just somebody no one would know.

(*DON JUAN clutches at his heart.*)

SECOND DAUGHTER: (*Smiles.*) Somebody you know, though, am I right?

(*DON JUAN is uncomfortably moved.*)

MOTHER: (*To the SECOND DAUGHTER.*) Don't be so cheeky! Go on, it's time you went, off you go!

SECOND DAUGHTER: (*Grins.*) Bye!

(*The SECOND DAUGHTER exits. DON JUAN is thinking about his fiancée.*)

DON JUAN: Bye.

(*Silence.*)

MOTHER: You can tell their father hasn't been here to bring them up. (*She sighs.*) So many sacrifices, so much suffering, and it just gets worse and worse. My husband was a university professor.

DON JUAN: (*Getting up.*) Well, then, I'll move in early tomorrow. I'm living in a boarding-house at the moment, but it's too noisy for me.

MOTHER: (*Getting up.*) I do hope you'll feel at home here... (*She gives DON JUAN her hand and stares at him suddenly, slowly.*) Tell me: haven't we met before?

DON JUAN: Could be...

(*DON JUAN takes his leave.*)

A Profiteer's House

FOUR LADIES are drinking tea. The FIRST LADY, a former governess, is the lady of the house and is thirty years old, the SECOND LADY, a film actress, twenty-three, the THIRD LADY is the girlfriend of a horse-dealer and the daughter of a concierge, eighteen; and the FOURTH LADY, a dentist, twenty-seven.

FIRST LADY: (*To the SECOND LADY.*) Lemon or rum?

SECOND LADY: Long as there's no sugar!

THIRD LADY: I couldn't exist without sugar.

SECOND LADY: Sugar makes you bosomy.

THIRD LADY: Rubbish.

FIRST LADY: Men still go for that, though. Get a big girl walking through a café, their eyes come out on stalks.

THIRD LADY: But you wouldn't catch them crossing the street with a big girl!

FOURTH LADY: You're all liars.

(*Silence.*)

FIRST LADY: I read a divine book yesterday about the psychology of Indian eroticism, all hand bound, it was. It's amazing, those Orientals, how magnificently inventive they are. Their ancient wisdom, they'll leave us all standing.

SECOND LADY: We're crazy about Asia as well at the moment, in the movies. That's all we ever do, exotic subjects, not counting the sex education films. I'm a princess in China, starting tomorrow.

THIRD LADY: (*Interrupting the SECOND LADY.*) Speaking of China, what's keeping him so long?

(*The FIRST LADY laughs.*)

FOURTH LADY: (*With a strange smile.*) He is sometimes a bit late...

SECOND LADY: Not for me.

(*The FOURTH LADY and the SECOND LADY exchange a look of hatred. The THIRD LADY is eating sugar.*)

THIRD LADY: He's always too early for me.

(*The FIRST LADY glances at the THIRD LADY with hatred.*)

FIRST LADY: (*To the SECOND LADY.*) Funny little thing, isn't she?

SECOND LADY: (*To the FIRST LADY.*) Wherever did you get that divine scarf, darling?

FIRST LADY: He gave it to me. Batik. That woodcut over there's from him as well...

SECOND LADY: Ah!

FIRST LADY: It's a St Sebastian.

(*The SECOND LADY gets up to look at the woodcut.*)

SECOND LADY: Fascinating use of perspective. Last time, when I had my chest trouble, he gave me a ceramic figure, Pan with his pipes.

THIRD LADY: What does he actually do?

SECOND LADY: (*Surprised.*) You mean you don't know?

THIRD LADY: Haven't a clue. I only know him, you know...

SECOND LADY: He's an art-dealer. (*To the FIRST LADY.*) By the way, not long ago he decided he wanted to go into films as well, I can't think who put that idea into his head, I did the best I could for him, but the test was a complete disaster.

FIRST LADY: (*Smiles.*) Yes, well, the best ones, they only work in the flesh.

THIRD LADY: (*Grins.*) Well, obviously.

FIRST LADY: (*Sighs ironically.*) Young girls nowadays, what's become of their ideals?

THIRD LADY: Ideals is for men. He's always telling me I remind him of some girl...

SECOND LADY: (*Dismissively.*) He's told me that as well.

FIRST LADY: We all remind him of somebody. With me it's her eyes, someone else it's her mouth...

THIRD LADY: Legs, I am.

SECOND LADY: (*To the FOURTH LADY, maliciously.*) What about you, darling?

(*The FOURTH LADY doesn't answer.*)

(*To the FIRST LADY.*) Probably her soul...

FIRST LADY: (*Smiles.*) Yes, well, he's trying to put the love of his life together, bit by bit.

FOURTH: LADY: (*Getting up suddenly.*) I can't stand this any more...
(*The FOURTH LADY paces nervously up and down.*)

THIRD LADY: (*To the SECOND LADY, puzzled.*) What's up with her, then?

FOURTH LADY: (*Stops abruptly.*) What's up with me? Do you still not understand or is it that you really don't want to understand, all he wants to do is degrade us...

FIRST LADY: (*Interrupting her, puzzled.*) Who?

FOURTH LADY: Him, him!

SECOND LADY: (*To the FOURTH LADY, mockingly.*) My dear child!

FOURTH LADY: (*Letting fly at the SECOND LADY.*) I am not a child, I'm a woman, and he really enjoys seeing us grovel, but the most horrible thing of all, is that we're degrading ourselves...

THIRD LADY: (*Eating sugar, contemptuously.*) It's too deep for me.

FOURTH LADY: Quite possibly.

THIRD LADY: Ow! My tooth...

SECOND LADY: Sugar, that'll be.

THIRD LADY: Oh...
(*The THIRD LADY holds her cheek.*)

FIRST LADY: (*Smiles.*) Does it hurt?

THIRD LADY: Like hell...

SECOND LADY: Happily we have a dentist among us
(*The SECOND LADY grins and points at the FOURTH LADY.*)

FOURTH LADY: (*To the THIRD LADY.*) Show me.
(*The THIRD LADY opens her mouth. The FOURTH LADY examines it.*)
It'll stop in a minute. Have you ever had rickets?

THIRD LADY: Me? Listen, what are you getting at, you? I've always had enough to eat, even in the great famine, I come from a decent home and my boyfriend was in the barbed-wire business, comprenez, you toothpick!

FIRST LADY: Ladies, please! I must ask you to bear in mind you're in the house of a corporation lawyer, who

for the last fortnight has been the government's
right-hand man...

THIRD LADY: (*Interrupting her.*) Yes, and who brought him
into the government? My friend! Who was it bribed both
the ministers?

FIRST LADY: (*Interrupting her.*) Will you be quiet! (*She looks
around nervously.*) The opposition have spies everywhere.
(*Silence.*)

FOURTH LADY: (*Disquietingly cold and clear.*) As soon as he
arrives, I'm going to tell him to his face what he is: the
scum of the earth.

SECOND LADY: Why? Because he doesn't want anything
more to do with you?

FOURTH LADY: (*Starting up.*) Who says?

SECOND LADY: He does.

(*The THIRD LADY laughs. The FOURTH LADY stares at
her.*)

FOURTH LADY: Does it still hurt?

THIRD LADY: (*Grim.*) It's okay.

FOURTH LADY: I see...mm, I pulled out one of his teeth
once, and he didn't bat an eyelid... He could put up with
anything...

(*The FOURTH LADY grins and suddenly throws herself on
to a sofa, weeping hysterically. The telephone rings. The FIRST
LADY answers it.*)

FIRST LADY: Hello. Yes? (*She pulls a long face.*) Really?
Thanks. (*She hangs up.*) He's sent a message saying he
can't come...

SECOND LADY: What?

FIRST LADY: He's stood us up.

THIRD LADY: Me?

FOURTH LADY: (*Laughs hysterically.*) Well done! Bravo!

THIRD LADY: (*To the FOURTH LADY.*) Shut up!

(*The FOURTH LADY falls silent and glares at the THIRD
LADY.*)

SECOND LADY: (*To the FIRST LADY.*) Where is he, then?

FIRST LADY: Probably with that cow from Berne again.
He sold her a Daumier yesterday, claims it's genuine.

(*The FOURTH LADY gets up and approaches the THIRD LADY slowly and menacingly.*)

SECOND LADY: Everything he achieves, he achieves because of us poor women.

(*The FOURTH LADY stops in front of the THIRD LADY.*)

FOURTH LADY: (*Quietly.*) Did you say shut up?

THIRD LADY: (*Looking the FOURTH LADY up and down disdainfully.*) Hysterical horseface...

FOURTH LADY: (*Yelling at her.*) Get out!

FIRST LADY: (*Screaming at the FOURTH LADY.*) Please, we don't want a scandal!

(*Silence.*)

THIRD LADY: See you in the mass grave!

(*The THIRD LADY exits quickly.*)

FIRST LADY: (*Murmuring to herself.*) Bye-bye.

Boxes at the Opera House

The previously mentioned LADY FROM BERNE in one, and an immensely FAT WOMAN, a butcher's wife dripping with diamonds, in the other. The opera is Mozart's 'Don Giovanni' and at the moment it's the duettino 'La ci darem la mano'. The LADY is very nervous, she keeps looking round while the FAT WOMAN sits motionless, staring at the stage through minute opera glasses. At the end of the duettino, DON JUAN steps into the LADY's box. He's wearing evening dress and kisses her hand. They speak very quietly.

LADY FROM BERNE: (*Breathing a sigh of relief.*) At last! I've been worried about you. My husband always keeps me waiting too.

DON JUAN: (*Sits down, smiling.*) Nothing to worry about.

(*Pause.*)

LADY FROM BERNE: Then where have you been?

DON JUAN: At the ice-rink.

LADY FROM BERNE: (*Puzzled.*) Where?

DON JUAN: One of my landlady's daughters, it's her birthday today, and I gave the child some skates. She just wanted to show me what she can do.

LADY FROM BERNE: And?

DON JUAN: She's a talented dancer. Potential world champion.

(*Pause.*)

LADY FROM BERNE: How old is this 'child', your future world champion?

DON JUAN: Fifteen.

(*The LADY FROM BERNE starts somewhat.*)

FAT WOMAN: (*Without taking her eyes off the stage.*) Sht!

(*Pause.*)

LADY FROM BERNE: Yesterday you sold me a Daumier, you know, a genuine Daumier?

DON JUAN: (*Looking up.*) Yes. Well?

LADY FROM BERNE: It's a fake.

DON JUAN: (*Surprised.*) What?

LADY FROM BERNE: I made enquiries.

(*Pause.*)

DON JUAN: When I got hold of it, it was guaranteed genuine...

LADY FROM BERNE: (*Interrupting him.*) I believe you implicitly, I'm sure you thought it was genuine...

(*Grins.*)

DON JUAN: I'll give you the money back, every penny...

(*DON JUAN rummages around in his wallet.*)

LADY FROM BERNE: I don't want anything back, do you understand?

FAT WOMAN: (*Without taking her eyes off the stage.*) Sht!

DON JUAN: (*Offering the LADY FROM BERNE a cheque.*) Here's your cheque. Take it...

LADY FROM BERNE: No.

DON JUAN: Take it.

LADY FROM BERNE: (*Staring at him wide-eyed.*) You have no soul.

DON JUAN: I'm not going to let you humiliate me. (*He holds the cheque out over the balcony, and lets it flutter down, watching its flight.*) It's down there now. Goodbye. Now it's worthless.

(*Pause.*)

LADY FROM BERNE: Satisfied?

DON JUAN: (*Loudly.*) Yes.

FAT WOMAN: Sht!

DON JUAN: (*To the FAT WOMAN.*) Forgive me.

> (*Only now does the FAT WOMAN catch sight of him. She stares at him, motionless. The LADY FROM BERNE points to the FAT WOMAN with a twisted smile.*)

LADY FROM BERNE: (*To DON JUAN.*) Your latest conquest...

DON JUAN: (*Grins.*) Don't tempt me.

> (*The Act is over, lights up, loud applause. The LADY FROM BERNE is holding her handkerchief in front of her eyes. The FAT WOMAN is still staring at DON JUAN. DON JUAN is on his feet, applauding.*)

At the Ice-Rink

It's closing-time, already late in the evening. The SECOND DAUGHTER is sitting on a bench in the open air with her schoolfriends, a BRUNETTE and a BLONDE. They're taking off their skates.

BRUNETTE: (*To the SECOND DAUGHTER.*) I envy you your new skates. I've always wanted a pair like that.

SECOND DAUGHTER: They're a birthday present.

BLONDE: Pity my birthday isn't till the summer, otherwise I'd get them to give me a pair like that. Must be heaven. (*Silence.*)

BRUNETTE: (*To the SECOND DAUGHTER.*) Who was that elegant man who was watching you earlier on?

SECOND DAUGHTER: He lives with us.

BLONDE: He was my type.

SECOND DAUGHTER: I don't think much of him.

BLONDE: Get on!

SECOND DAUGHTER: No, I don't like him any more.

BLONDE: Come on, I saw you, you were trying three times as hard, when he was watching.

SECOND DAUGHTER: (*Looking up.*) Funny, I thought I never really got going...

BRUNETTE: You were firm as a rock!

SECOND DAUGHTER: I wobbled...

BLONDE: (*Interrupting her.*) You've never skated as well in your life!

SECOND DAUGHTER: (*Smiles sarcastically.*) You should know.

(*Silence.*)

BRUNETTE: What's he done to put you off him?

SECOND DAUGHTER: Nothing. It's just I had a dream about him a few nights ago.

BLONDE: Is that all?

SECOND DAUGHTER: He killed me.

BLONDE: How?

SECOND DAUGHTER: You know the wood over there, I was walking through it, near that bend in the path where that weird tree is, it was dark, and I suddenly felt his hand, except his fingers were all knives...no, I don't like thinking about it, it was too horrible! I'd been awake a long time and I still thought I was dead.

BLONDE: (*Laughs.*) Here you are, though!

SECOND DAUGHTER: (*Smiles.*) Hope so.

(*A dull rumble in the distance.*)

BRUNETTE: (*Listens.*) The ice is cracking.

SECOND DAUGHTER: It'll be even colder tomorrow.

BLONDE: Come on! The gates are shut already, they'll be locking us in!

The Mother's Spare Room

DON JUAN is having breakfast in his furnished room. He's wearing dark pyjamas. The MOTHER silently opens the door, creeps up behind him and all of a sudden puts her hands over his eyes.

MOTHER: Cuckoo! Cuckoo! Guess who?

DON JUAN: (*Grins.*) No idea...

MOTHER: (*Taking her hands away.*) You devil...nice breakfast?

DON JUAN: Very.

MOTHER: There's a letter for you...

DON JUAN: (*Interrupting her.*) Where from?

MOTHER: (*Giving him the letter.*) What are you so afraid of?

DON JUAN: Can't remember...

(*DON JUAN smiles, opens the letter and reads it.*)

MOTHER: It's from a woman. May I read it?

DON JUAN: No.

(*Silence.*)

MOTHER: You have secrets from me?

DON JUAN: Yes.

(*Silence.*

The MOTHER suddenly snatches it out of his hand.)

DON JUAN: Give it back at once.

MOTHER: Wouldn't dream of it...

(*The MOTHER reads it quickly and looks at DON JUAN, aghast.*)

DON JUAN: (*Smiles.*) Satisfied now, are you?

MOTHER: (*Pointing to the letter.*) Is that the kind of man you are?

DON JUAN: So they say.

MOTHER: Is it true?

DON JUAN: I don't accept any responsibility.

MOTHER: A woman saying she's going to drown herself because of you...

DON JUAN: (*Interrupting her.*) She'll change her mind.

MOTHER: God, the way you talk!

DON JUAN: Is it my fault I don't find her attractive any more? What am I supposed to do, force myself?

MOTHER: Now you're frightening me.

DON JUAN: (*Smiles.*) Nothing to be afraid of. (*He takes the letter back from her.*) She's a designer, she asked me to dance. She insisted until she got what she wanted. Full stop. We met a few times, and then I realised I was wrong about her. (*He grins.*) Originally, you see, she reminded me of someone, but there turned out to be no similarities, it was just a poetic fantasy of mine. Yes, that's always happening. I just can't seem to find it, my ideal...

(*DON JUAN laughs.*)

MOTHER: You'll never find it, because you don't have an ideal any more. It's dead.

DON JUAN: (*Taken aback.*) Dead? (*He clutches at his heart.*)
No...no, that's impossible! I'm sure she's alive somewhere
and married to some honest man. She has children and
wants to be left in peace, that's why she hasn't answered
me...
(*DON JUAN grins.*)
MOTHER: I can understand that.
DON JUAN: (*Suddenly letting fly at her.*) I'll tell you what
you can understand! What you see, what you hear and
what you taste! Who do you think you are, anyway? Just
some nice civil service widow who thinks every time she
gives herself to a man, that moment a star's going to fall
out of the sky!
MOTHER: Don't forget, I'm only human!
DON JUAN: But I want to forget! I don't want to be
reminded any more! That's enough!
(*Silence.*)
MOTHER: Where you sleep, that was his bed...do you
understand? And it's his desk you write at and his
clothes that used to hang in that wardrobe before I had
to sell them... I've often seen him sitting here at this
desk, even after he was killed, and even if I didn't see
him, I knew he was in the room, watching me, as if time
didn't exist. You, it's only you who've driven him out.
You be careful he doesn't come back, that he's not out
there standing in the corridor when I've gone... (*She
moves closer to DON JUAN.*) Listen, I don't ever want to see
him again, never, never again... (*She presses herself against
him.*) Leave me alone, please, let me go...
DON JUAN: (*Not moving.*) I'm not touching you.
(*The MOTHER suddenly lets go of him and clutches her
head as if only now were she forced to come to her senses.*)
MOTHER: What is it that attracts me to you?
DON JUAN: Nothing.
MOTHER: (*Dully.*) That's right, nothing. (*She shouts at him.*)
What are you doing to me?
DON JUAN: Nothing. (*He shouts at her.*) So for God's sake
leave me in peace!
(*Silence.*)

MOTHER: (*With hatred.*) I'm leaving you. I'm leaving you...
(*The MOTHER exits. DON JUAN is alone. He stares after her.*)
DON JUAN: About time.

The Designers' Studio

The Two DESIGNERS come into their small studio. The FIRST DESIGNER is completely drunk, and the SECOND DESIGNER turns the light on, it's already far into the night.

FIRST DESIGNER: (*Sings.*) Who'll weep for us, when we part...
SECOND DESIGNER: (*Interrupting her in an undertone.*) Be quiet! Go to bed...
FIRST DESIGNER: Why should I?
(*The FIRST DESIGNER tries to pour out some schnapps. The SECOND DESIGNER takes the bottle from her.*)
I'm not drunk...
SECOND DESIGNER: You've had enough.
(*Silence.
Suddenly, the FIRST DESIGNER shouts at the SECOND DESIGNER.*)
FIRST DESIGNER: I have not had enough!
SECOND DESIGNER: Not so loud! The neighbours'll...
FIRST DESIGNER: (*Interrupting her, yelling.*) I want some more, I want some more!
(*The FIRST DESIGNER snatches the bottle out of her hand. The neighbours bang on the wall.*)
SECOND DESIGNER: Hear that? They'll throw us out.
FIRST DESIGNER: (*Pours a drink; quietly.*) I don't care.
SECOND DESIGNER: Well, I do! You know it's impossible finding anywhere to live nowadays...
FIRST DESIGNER: I could sleep on a pile of manure. (*She drinks and suddenly bursts into bitter tears.*) It's your fault he doesn't want anything to do with me, or like me any more...
SECOND DESIGNER: (*Puzzled.*) My fault?

FIRST DESIGNER: He tore up my letters and I thought he would save me...

SECOND DESIGNER: (*Scornfully.*) Save you?

FIRST DESIGNER: Yes, from you.

(*The FIRST DESIGNER looks at her gravely and then laughs at her quietly.*

Silence.

The SECOND DESIGNER nods her head sadly.)

SECOND DESIGNER: You'll always come whining back to me...

FIRST DESIGNER: (*Shouting at her again.*) Come whining back to you, like hell I will! You told me curls are effeminate and lace is effeminate and high heels are effeminate and I wore what you wanted me to, the way you wanted me to, but now, now I've had enough of it! (*She rips off her dress shirt and throws it at the feet of the SECOND DESIGNER.*) That's what I think of your taste in fashion!

(*The neighbours bang on the wall again, this time noticeably louder. The SECOND DESIGNER doesn't hear the banging, just stares at the FIRST DESIGNER.*)

SECOND DESIGNER: (*Dully.*) Peter, Peter...

FIRST DESIGNER: (*Screaming.*) My name is not Peter! My name is Alice!

(*Silence.*)

SECOND DESIGNER: Goodbye, Alice...

(*The SECOND DESIGNER moves off abruptly.*)

FIRST DESIGNER: (*Surprised.*) Where are you going?

SECOND DESIGNER: For a walk.

FIRST DESIGNER: (*With hatred.*) Aren't you ready for bed?

SECOND DESIGNER: (*Letting fly at her.*) Sleep by yourself! (*The SECOND DESIGNER exits.*)

(*The FIRST DESIGNER, alone, drinks and undresses.*)

FIRST DESIGNER: By myself? No, I'm never sleeping by myself again. (*She looks around.*) Where are you, you bastard? (*She fetches a photograph of DON JUAN out of a drawer.*) Ah, there you are. (*She puts the photograph on the table, sits down and contemplates it.*) How are you? All right? Me too. (*She laughs.*) Now, listen to this: our child is gone, that's right, gone, vanished, and I can never have another, never again, you got that? Tough luck... I wrote and told you I'd drown myself if you didn't come, that'd suit you, wouldn't it? Just look at me. Who was it I reminded you of, mm? Go on, tell me, who was the bitch? Who was she? (*She jumps up.*) Don't you look at me like that! You just wait... (*She takes a needle, pokes the photograph's eyes out and puts it back on the table.*) All right, now try looking at me... What? You're still looking? (*She yells at the photograph.*) Stop looking at me, stop it! (*She grabs a chair and lashes out furiously at the table where the photograph is standing, smashing glasses and plates.*) There, there, there!

(*The neighbours are banging very loudly on the walls and a furious female voice shouts: 'Be quiet!'*
The FIRST DESIGNER leans against the wall, exhausted.
A NEIGHBOUR appears in her nightgown.)

NEIGHBOUR: (*Scolding.*) What's all this noise when people are trying to sleep? What's the matter with you, Fräulein?

FIRST DESIGNER: (*Smiles stupidly; slowly.*) I've just murdered someone...

NEIGHBOUR: Jesus and Mary!

(*The NEIGHBOUR crosses herself.*)

The Mother's Spare Room

DON JUAN paces up and down in his furnished room. It's the afternoon and he's expecting a visitor. A small table has been laid. He looks at his watch, there's a knock at the door and the SECOND DAUGHTER comes in. DON JUAN is surprised. The SECOND DAUGHTER looks at him seriously.

SECOND DAUGHTER: I wanted to ask you a big favour.

DON JUAN: (*Smiles.*) Be brave.

SECOND DAUGHTER: You'll be angry...

DON JUAN: (*Interrupting her.*) I'm never angry.

SECOND DAUGHTER: Cross your heart?

DON JUAN: If you like. Well?

(*Silence.*)

SECOND DAUGHTER: Please don't come to the ice-rink any more...

DON JUAN: (*Surprised.*) Why not?

SECOND DAUGHTER: (*Looks at him, wide-eyed.*) I don't want you watching me any more, please...

(*Silence.*)

DON JUAN: Why shouldn't I, if I enjoy it?

SECOND DAUGHTER: Because I'm no good at it.

DON JUAN: You're very talented, my dear. You'll finish up a world champion.

SECOND DAUGHTER: Not if you keep watching me, that's for sure.

(*Silence.*)

DON JUAN: Well, no one's ever said that to me before...

SECOND DAUGHTER: (*Interrupting him.*) Promise me you won't come any more?

DON JUAN: I'll do my best, but I never make promises.

(*Silence.*)

SECOND DAUGHTER: Should I give you back the skates?

DON JUAN: (*Looks up and stares at her.*) Whose idea is this? Your mother's?

SECOND DAUGHTER: She wants me to as well, but that doesn't count.

DON JUAN: Then what does count? Aren't I allowed to give someone a present?

(*Silence.*)

SECOND DAUGHTER: (*Slowly.*) I'll keep your skates...

DON JUAN: (*Ironically.*) Thanks very much.

SECOND DAUGHTER: (*Smiles mysteriously.*) But if I fall through the ice and drown, it'll be your fault...

DON JUAN: Of course.

(*The doorbell rings. DON JUAN looks up, glances at the table, which is laid.*)

SECOND DAUGHTER: Are you expecting someone?

DON JUAN: (*Smiles.*) I suppose I am...

SECOND DAUGHTER: Another woman?

DON JUAN: She invited herself...

(*DON JUAN sets off to answer the door.*)

SECOND DAUGHTER: I'll do it!

(*The SECOND DAUGHTER exits quickly. DON JUAN, alone, automatically straightens his tie in the mirror.*)

DON JUAN: That's right, it's always your fault...

(*DON JUAN laughs shortly. The SECOND DAUGHTER comes back.*)

Well?

SECOND DAUGHTER: She's gone away again.

DON JUAN: (*Surprised.*) Why?

SECOND DAUGHTER: I sent her.

(*Silence.*)

DON JUAN: Well, it's no skin off my nose...

(*DON JUAN grins.*)

SECOND DAUGHTER: (*Suddenly shouting at him.*) You're not to have any more visitors, the walls are thin, I can't bear it, I can hear every word, it's killing me!

(*Silence.*

DON JUAN pours himself some coffee and drinks. The SECOND DAUGHTER watches him.)

(*Quietly.*) I wouldn't like to be in your shoes.

DON JUAN: Really...

(*DON JUAN eats a cake.*)

SECOND DAUGHTER: If I were you, I wouldn't want to go on living.

DON JUAN: (*Bows, laughing.*) Well, now I know. Like some coffee?

SECOND DAUGHTER: I don't want anything from you!

(*The SECOND DAUGHTER gives a sob and exits quickly. DON JUAN, alone, stares after her.*)

DON JUAN: You just wait till you're older...

(*DON JUAN grins.*)

End of Act Two.

ACT THREE: The Snowman

The Stairwell

The FIRST DAUGHTER waits in the stairwell for DON JUAN's return. It's a pitch-black winter's night and the space is lit only by the rays of a street-lamp. Finally DON JUAN unlocks the front door; he's come from a masked ball with a MASKED LADY, the young wife of a businessman. DON JUAN turns the light on. The FIRST DAUGHTER becomes visible. The MASKED LADY, although she hasn't noticed the FIRST DAUGHTER, screams.

MASKED LADY: Turn the light off! My husband'll kill me if he sees me!
(*DON JUAN, who hasn't seen the FIRST DAUGHTER either, turns the light off again.*)
DON JUAN: Nobody'll see you here. Come on, it's not far up...
MASKED LADY: (*Stopping suddenly.*) What am I doing with you?
DON JUAN: (*Smiles.*) Don't you know?
MASKED LADY: I can't.
DON JUAN: (*Puzzled.*) What?
(*Silence.*)
MASKED LADY: Is it a surprise, to be refused by a beautiful masked lady?
DON JUAN: You talk like a good novel.
MASKED LADY: I'm not a novel.
DON JUAN: Come on...
MASKED LADY: No. At the moment I don't feel anything for you...
DON JUAN: You're making a terrible mistake.
MASKED LADY: Everything about you is dead, it's as if there was glass between us, a thick piece of glass you could stand on without it cracking... Let go of me, please! You belong to another!

DON JUAN: I don't belong to anyone.

MASKED LADY: I don't want to take you away from someone. You'll be grateful to me sometime for not...

DON JUAN: (*Interrupting her.*) Grateful? When? On the Day of Judgement?

MASKED LADY: Perhaps then we'll meet again.

DON JUAN: (*Grins.*) No doubt.

(*Silence.*)

MASKED LADY: Well, then, let me out...

(*DON JUAN opens the front door.*)

(*Hesitating.*) You let me go as easy as that?

DON JUAN: I never force myself on anyone. I'll get over you...

(*DON JUAN smiles and clutches at his heart.*)

MASKED LADY: Bastard!

(*The MASKED LADY exits quickly. DON JUAN closes the front door, turns the light on, and is surprised when he catches sight of the FIRST DAUGHTER.*)

DON JUAN: What are you doing hanging about here?

FIRST DAUGHTER: Waiting for you. For the last hour, I'm waiting here because my mother's not supposed to know anything about what we're going to discuss and I never have time during the day.

DON JUAN: Is it to do with your mother?

FIRST DAUGHTER: No. It's to do with something a great deal more important. I need money. I find it very hard to ask you, but I'm more than prepared to overcome my scruples, because one of my comrades' welfare is at stake and you're the only capitalist I know...

(*The FIRST DAUGHTER smiles sarcastically.*)

DON JUAN: You have a false impression of me.

(*DON JUAN smiles.*)

FIRST DAUGHTER: My comrade has participated in a revolutionary act and there's a warrant out for her. She needs a passport. Please help me. It's urgent.

DON JUAN: Mm. What'll happen to her if I don't help?

FIRST DAUGHTER: Prison.

DON JUAN: That's bad. Is she pretty?

FIRST DAUGHTER: (*Surprised.*) Who?

DON JUAN: Your comrade...

FIRST DAUGHTER: (*Staring at him.*) The things you ask...

DON JUAN: (*Interrupting her.*) Most natural question in the world.

FIRST DAUGHTER: It's obvious you know nothing about the appalling sufferings of the broad masses...

DON JUAN: Masses, masses! I wondered when that was coming!

FIRST DAUGHTER: You'd better get used to it! It's true your world still rules, thanks to terror, murder and oppression...

DON JUAN: (*Interrupting her.*) My world?

FIRST DAUGHTER: Yes, you trampled down the revolution, but we're on the way back!

DON JUAN: I've never trampled down anyone, there must be some mistake. You seem to take me for a rising force. (*DON JUAN smiles.*)

FIRST DAUGHTER: I'm not talking about you personally...

DON JUAN: (*Interrupting her.*) That's a pity. A great pity.

FIRST DAUGHTER: Stop all this nonsense. You're a product of your class as much as anyone else, and there are only two classes: exploiters and exploited, and you...

DON JUAN: (*Interrupting her again.*) I've always been exploited.

FIRST DAUGHTER: (*Scornfully.*) By whom?

DON JUAN: By you. Women. But I get my own back. All those of you I don't find attractive...just don't exist for me as people.

FIRST DAUGHTER: So for you, a woman only begins to exist as a person providing she has the money to be able to tart herself up? I sit in an office and I hardly earn anything. And what about all those millions in the factories who wither away while they're still young... I suppose you have no sympathy at all for any of them?

DON JUAN: No. I wouldn't go so far as to say that.

FIRST DAUGHTER: You're a hereditary criminal.

DON JUAN: Just as you like.

FIRST DAUGHTER: The relationship between the sexes is not a problem for us any more, it's just a function, like eating and drinking!

DON JUAN: (*Ironically.*) How interesting.

FIRST DAUGHTER: There are no secrets any more! We've gone beyond all that.

DON JUAN: And where have you arrived?

(*The FIRST DAUGHTER looks startled and stares at DON JUAN.*)

Just look at yourself in the mirror.

FIRST DAUGHTER: I'm not vain.

DON JUAN: You're an ugly girl. All the same I'm going to help your comrade... (*He grins and gives her a bundle of banknotes.*) Bon voyage!

(*The FIRST DAUGHTER takes the bundle from him and keeps staring at DON JUAN.*)

FIRST DAUGHTER: (*Dully.*) You animal...

DON JUAN: Is that all the thanks I get?

FIRST DAUGHTER: Why do you have to torment me?

DON JUAN: Because I find you offensive.

(*DON JUAN leaves the FIRST DAUGHTER there and goes up the stairs.*

The FIRST DAUGHTER, alone, sits down on the bottom step, counts the money mechanically and suddenly bursts into tears.)

The Mother's Spare Room

In his room, DON JUAN is taking off his tails. He's smoking a cigarette. The MOTHER enters, she's beside herself.

MOTHER: I have to speak to you at once.

DON JUAN: What?

MOTHER: You've been at the ice-rink again, this evening...

DON JUAN: Yes.

MOTHER: And you walked back some of the way with Gretl...through the wood, isn't that right?

DON JUAN: So?

(*The MOTHER looks at DON JUAN, wide-eyed, and suddenly bursts violently into tears.*)

(*Touching her arm.*) What's the matter?

MOTHER: (*Screaming.*) Don't touch me! Don't touch me, you criminal! You've seduced my child...

DON JUAN: What? Me?

MOTHER: You raped my child!

DON JUAN: I did what to your child? Who says?

MOTHER: She does!

DON JUAN: She's lying, she's lying!

MOTHER: You're the liar, you are! I know you all right!

DON JUAN: (*Stares at her; quietly.*) You must be insane...

MOTHER: (*Glares at him full of hatred.*) You're guilty. She confessed everything to me.

DON JUAN: Where is she? She'd better come and say all this to my face!

MOTHER: You're not going to see her again. Not until you get to court.

(*Silence.*)

DON JUAN: I swear to you, by everything that's holy...

MOTHER: (*Laughs.*) Nothing's holy to you any more. Not to you!

DON JUAN: (*Shouting at her.*) I swear blind!

(*The SECOND DAUGHTER enters, distraught and tearful.*)

MOTHER: (*Screaming.*) Go away! Get out!

(*DON JUAN moves quickly to block the door.*)

DON JUAN: Wait! (*To the SECOND DAUGHTER.*) What is it I've done?

SECOND DAUGHTER: (*Gazing at him nervously.*) You gave me some skates...

DON JUAN: And?

SECOND DAUGHTER: You're always looking at my legs.

MOTHER: (*Letting fly at her.*) Will you go now?

(*She grabs hold of the SECOND DAUGHTEr's arm and pinches her.*)

SECOND DAUGHTER: Ow! Let go! (*She wrenches herself free and gazes at DON JUAN again, fascinated.*) You put your hand over my mouth...

63

DON JUAN: Your mouth?

SECOND DAUGHTER: In the wood, near that bend in the path. You stood me up against a tree. You wanted to tie me up... (*She shouts at DON JUAN.*) You beat me!

DON JUAN: Lies, lies, lies!

SECOND DAUGHTER: I don't want to go on living! Why didn't you kill me?

(*DON JUAN stares at the SECOND DAUGHTER, incredulous, then quickly puts on his tails and his overcoat. The MOTHER watches him and blocks the door.*)

MOTHER: Where d'you think you're going? I'm not letting you get away...

DON JUAN: All this has got to be sorted out. I'm going to the police.

MOTHER: I don't believe you!

DON JUAN: You ought to be ashamed of yourself. Out of the way! (*He exits.*)

MOTHER: (*Shouting after him.*) I'll see you hanged!

(*The SECOND DAUGHTER looks at her legs, sobbing.*)

The Profiteer's House

The FIRST LADY, the lady of the house, is drinking her tea on her own. The SECOND LADY, the film actress, enters with a newspaper, excited.

SECOND LADY: Have you read it yet? The devil's come to fetch him at last.

FIRST LADY: Who?

SECOND LADY: Our great lover... (*She laughs maliciously and hands the FIRST LADY the newspaper.*) His latest girl's under age...

FIRST LADY: Aha.

SECOND LADY: It was bound to happen.

FIRST LADY: (*Reading avidly.*) He's finished.

SECOND LADY: He went to the Police himself and denied it outright, but they don't believe the man is innocent... (*She grins.*) His reputation's not too good.

FIRST LADY: (*Reading.*) Even if he is innocent, he deserves everything he gets.

SECOND LADY: They were going to arrest him today, but he seems to have found it preferable to disappear… (*She pours herself some tea.*) He hasn't a hope. There's a warrant out for him.

FIRST LADY: (*Still reading.*) Are they on to him yet?

SECOND LADY: They're still groping around in the dark, but they'll get him. There's no room in this world for men like him.

FIRST LADY: Yes, it's a small world… (*Her eyes fall on an advertisement in the newspaper.*) By the way, have you seen 'The Maharajah's Favourite'?

SECOND LADY: It's an enchanting film! Full of the most amazing stuff!

The Forest Deep in Snow

Two OLD WOMEN enter with bundles of wood on their backs. Dusk.

FIRST OLD WOMAN: (*Muted.*) Don't move! There's somebody there!
(*Both OLD WOMEN listen.*)

SECOND OLD WOMAN: I can't hear a thing. I can't see a thing.

FIRST OLD WOMAN: I thought I heard something moving about…
(*Both OLD WOMEN listen some more.*)

SECOND OLD WOMAN: The gamekeeper chased me off yesterday, threatened to put the police on me…

FIRST OLD WOMAN: The gamekeeper should be miles away by now.

SECOND OLD WOMAN: All because of a little bit of wood. He says it's stealing… The nobs in town, what they get up to, I hate to think what he calls that!

FIRST OLD WOMAN: (*Looking round.*) Who owns this forest, anyway?

SECOND OLD WOMAN: I don't know what he calls himself. Some big racketeer, must be...

FIRST OLD WOMAN: That's right, the world's going from bad to worse.

(*DON JUAN suddenly appears; he looks weather-beaten. The TWO OLD WOMEN are frightened. DON JUAN looks at them suspiciously.*)

SECOND OLD WOMAN: (*Subdued.*) Evening, sir.

DON JUAN: (*Looking round.*) Am I heading in the right direction? I'm looking for the station...

SECOND OLD WOMAN: There's no station here. The nearest is a good three hours away.

DON JUAN: It'll pass.

(*DON JUAN starts to set off.*)

SECOND OLD WOMAN: You'll have to go across the marshes, I wouldn't do that when it's dark.

DON JUAN: It'll all be frozen over.

FIRST OLD WOMAN: The marshes never freeze over, and they'll suck you down, sir, unless you know where God lives.

DON JUAN: (*Looking up.*) And where does he live?

SECOND OLD WOMAN: (*Laughs; to DON JUAN.*) She knows! She knows all right!

FIRST OLD WOMAN: (*To the SECOND OLD WOMAN.*) I do know, I do too!

SECOND OLD WOMAN: (*Letting fly at the FIRST OLD WOMAN.*) Well, I don't believe in anything! Not any more!

(*Silence.*)

DON JUAN: (*To the FIRST OLD WOMAN.*) Tell me, do you speak to him sometimes, God, I mean?

FIRST OLD WOMAN: Yes.

SECOND OLD WOMAN: (*Grins.*) Every morning and evening.

DON JUAN: (*To the FIRST OLD WOMAN.*) Then give him my regards, will you, nobody'll believe that I've been falsely accused and I'm innocent...

FIRST OLD WOMAN: (*Staring at DON JUAN, almost frightened.*) May I ask, innocent of what?

DON JUAN: He'll know about it already...
(*DON JUAN exits.*
The TWO OLD WOMEN watch him go, surprised.)
SECOND OLD WOMAN: (*Suddenly calling after him.*) Bon
voyage, sir, bon voyage!
(*The SECOND OLD WOMAN laughs.*)

The Snowman

The moon shines down on a snowman in the village. TWO VILLAGE
GIRLS enter.

FIRST VILLAGE GIRL: Look at the snowman!
SECOND VILLAGE GIRL: My brother built that. Come
on, let's knock his arm off, that'll upset him...
(*The SECOND VILLAGE GIRL picks up a stick and knocks*
the snowman's right arm off.)
FIRST VILLAGE GIRL: I'll bash his head in!
(*The FIRST VILLAGE GIRL does so. DON JUAN enters.*
The TWO VILLAGE GIRLS are a bit frightened.)
DON JUAN: How do I get to the station?
FIRST VILLAGE GIRL: That way.
SECOND VILLAGE GIRL: Do you want to go tonight?
DON JUAN: Yes.
SECOND VILLAGE GIRL: There's no more trains today,
the last one's already gone.
DON JUAN: Has it? (*He looks round.*) Where can you spend
the night here?
FIRST VILLAGE GIRL: At the inn.
DON JUAN: And apart from the inn?
FIRST VILLAGE GIRL: (*Shrugging her shoulders.*) Nowhere.
DON JUAN: Ah.
(*DON JUAN reflects.*
Silence.
The Two VILLAGE GIRLS whisper to one another.)
SECOND VILLAGE GIRL: (*Insolently.*) Why don't you
want to spend the night at the inn, then? Are you in
trouble?
DON JUAN: (*Starting slightly.*) Me? (*He clutches at his heart.*)
Why should I be?

SECOND VILLAGE GIRL: We know all about that. Our dad was in trouble once and he wouldn't go near an inn, because he was afraid of having to register...
(*The SECOND VILLAGE GIRL grins.*)
FIRST VILLAGE GIRL: (*Matter-of-fact.*) He froze to death in the forest.
(*DON JUAN stares at them.*)
SECOND VILLAGE GIRL: It was ages ago. A year and a half.
(*The SECOND VILLAGE GIRL bashes the snowman on the head. The FIRST VILLAGE GIRL knocks his left arm off.*)
DON JUAN: What harm's the snowman done to you?
FIRST VILLAGE GIRL: None. It's the bloke who built him...
SECOND VILLAGE GIRL: He'll be gone tomorrow anyway.
FIRST VILLAGE GIRL: It's getting warmer.
(*The FIRST VILLAGE GIRL bashes away at the snowman.*)

Room at the Inn

DON JUAN fills in the registration form. Then he rings. The LANDLADY enters, she's very chatty and nosey.

DON JUAN: The registration form...
(*DON JUAN gives it to her.*)
LANDLADY: Thank you very much. (*She looks at the form.*) Commercial traveller are you, sir?
DON JUAN: Yes. And please wake me very early tomorrow, so I don't miss the first train.
LANDLADY: (*Interrupting him.*) Why d'you want to take the first train? It's really miserable, you'd do better to go on the second, I'm not saying that because of the breakfast, I don't make anything on that!
DON JUAN: If I take the second, I'll miss my connection.
LANDLADY: Oh, you're travelling on, are you?
DON JUAN: I'm on my way to get married...
(*DON JUAN smiles.*)

LANDLADY: (*Surprised.*) You'd better lie down, then!
Where does she live, your fiancée?

DON JUAN: We haven't seen each other for ages.

LANDLADY: Why's that?

DON JUAN: It's my profession, it's kept me busy...
(*DON JUAN smiles again.*)

LANDLADY: Yes, well, we all have our cross to bear! So,
anyway, you'll have plenty to talk about...

DON JUAN: A great deal.

LANDLADY: Soon, is it, the wedding?

DON JUAN: (*Grins.*) Maybe...

LANDLADY: That's right, well done!
(*DON JUAN clutches at his heart and buckles slightly.*)
What's up, then?

DON JUAN: (*Quietly.*) Just a pain...

LANDLADY: You want to watch out for that, it's no joke,
your heart!

DON JUAN: (*Sitting down.*) Could I have a glass of water?

LANDLADY: Shan't be a minute, got to look after the
bridegroom!
(*The LANDLADY exits.*)

In Front of the Grandmother's House

*In the small town, in front of the GRANDMOTHER's house. It's
still day, but the sun's rays can't penetrate the mist. Deep snow
everywhere. TWO LITTLE GIRLS with their satchels on their backs
are standing in front of the iron gate which leads to the front garden;
they ring the bell loudly and then hide.*

MAID: (*Opening the front door.*) Anyone there? Hello? (*She
shouts.*) Who's there?
(*The TWO LITTLE GIRLS giggle quietly.*)
(*Looking round.*) Must be those grubby little brats again!
Trying to annoy the old witch and keep me on the go!
(*The MAID exits, furious.*)

FIRST LITTLE GIRL: (*To the SECOND LITTLE GIRL.*)
Your turn!

SECOND LITTLE GIRL: I'll give it a good ring...
*(She does so and runs back to hide with the FIRST LITTLE
GIRL. Silence.*
*The GRANDMOTHER appears at the front door, leaning
on her stick; she looks round warily.)*
GRANDMOTHER: *(Quietly.)* Who is that? I'll pull your
ears off, I'll kill you... Riff-raff, scum...just try it once
more, that's all.
*(The GRANDMOTHER flourishes her stick threateningly
and exits. Silence.)*
FIRST LITTLE GIRL: *(To the SECOND LITTLE GIRL.)* Go
on, do it again!
SECOND LITTLE GIRL: No, it's your turn!
FIRST LITTLE GIRL: I've done it twice already...
*(She suddenly breaks off, frightened and points furtively down
the street.)*
Look out! There's a man coming!
(DON JUAN enters and stops.)
DON JUAN: Tell me: which is number six?
*(The SECOND LITTLE GIRL points to the
GRANDMOTHER's house.)*
SECOND LITTLE GIRL: That one.
DON JUAN: *(Looking round uncertainly.)* Doesn't it say?
FIRST LITTLE GIRL: The number's covered with snow...
*(The FIRST LITTLE GIRL runs off with the SECOND
LITTLE GIRL. DON JUAN watches them go and rings the
bell. Silence.*
*DON JUAN rings again. The GRANDMOTHER appears
at the front door, shaking with rage.)*
GRANDMOTHER: *(Shrieking.)* Who's that, who's that
ringing? Who's that never leaves me in peace?
*(The GRANDMOTHER catches sight of DON JUAN and
stops short.)*
DON JUAN: Excuse me, is this number six?
GRANDMOTHER: *(Examining him suspiciously.)* What do
you want? I don't need anything, I've got everything!
DON JUAN: *(Smiles.)* I'm not a beggar. I'd like to speak to
the young lady.

(*The GRANDMOTHER stares at DON JUAN, frightened.*)
Is she at home?
(*The GRANDMOTHER just stares at DON JUAN.*)
I was wondering if she was at home?
GRANDMOTHER: (*Dully.*) You're looking for my granddaughter?
DON JUAN: (*A slight bow.*) Yes.
GRANDMOTHER: Who shall I say it is, please?
DON JUAN: (*Smiles.*) I was hoping to surprise her...
(*Silence.*)
GRANDMOTHER: I know who you are.
(*DON JUAN starts and clutches at his heart.*)
DON JUAN: Where is she?
GRANDMOTHER: Later. What is it you want from her now?
(*Silence.*)
DON JUAN: (*Slowly.*) I came here to tell her, you ought not to keep a man waiting so long, you ought to feel some responsibility towards someone who wants to reform...
GRANDMOTHER: (*Interrupting him.*) You dare to say that, you!
DON JUAN: Yes, I know I was a bastard! But I wanted to put things right...
GRANDMOTHER: (*Interrupting him with hatred.*) It's too late for that!
DON JUAN: I don't want to any more! Everything would have been different, if she'd answered!
GRANDMOTHER: (*Scornfully.*) Hardly!
DON JUAN: Of course it would! So where is she? I just want to see what it was tied me to her so strongly I couldn't ever take on any other ties...and what still ties me! I can't even remember what she looks like!
(*DON JUAN clutches at his heart and turns pale.*)
GRANDMOTHER: (*Watching him.*) What's the matter with you?
DON JUAN: (*Quietly.*) I'm not supposed to get excited!
GRANDMOTHER: Oh, really?
(*The GRANDMOTHER grins. Silence.*)

DON JUAN: (*Slowly, quietly.*) Tell me: is there someone else?

(*Silence.*)

GRANDMOTHER: The girl you're looking for is dead.

(*DON JUAN stares at the GRANDMOTHER, aghast.*)

She passed away. On the third of March, nineteen-sixteen.

DON JUAN: Passed away...

(*Silence.*)

GRANDMOTHER: She wanted to die. There was someone who felt no responsibility towards her, a bastard. Do you still know how to pray?

(*Silence.*)

DON JUAN: The third of March nineteen-sixteen...so she never read my letters?

GRANDMOTHER: No. I did.

(*DON JUAN looks round, as if he were being followed.*)

Are you afraid?

DON JUAN: Yes.

GRANDMOTHER: The dead are peaceable, they leave us be... (*The GRANDMOTHER grins again.*)

DON JUAN: (*Staring at her.*) Take care. You may be having a visitor soon...

(*The GRANDMOTHER starts and gazes at him terrified.*)

GRANDMOTHER: (*Shrieking suddenly.*) Anna! Anna!

(*The MAID appears at the front door.*)

Show this gentleman where the grave is! He's a distant relation...

DON JUAN: I'll find my own way.

GRANDMOTHER: No, you could get lost.

Cemetery

DON JUAN enters with the MAID. Dusk.

MAID: The young lady's here.

(*DON JUAN steps up to the grave and contemplates it.*)

(*Looking up at the sky.*) There's more snow on the way.

(*Silence.*)

DON JUAN: (*Uncertainly.*) Tell me: she didn't do anything to herself, did she?

MAID: Whatever gave you that idea? No, poor thing, she just died, all by herself. She was in great pain and she cried all day and all night, and then suddenly she started to laugh and then she laughed all day and all night. It was terrible, I can still hear it, the way it was when they came to take her away...

DON JUAN: Where to?

MAID: The Good Shepherd.

DON JUAN: What's that?

MAID: A private asylum.

(*It's starting to snow, more and more heavily.*)

My sister's over there. I'll just go over and say an Our Father, I won't be a minute...

(*The MAID exits. DON JUAN is alone; he speaks to his dead bride.*)

DON JUAN: Do you get cold, when it snows like this? Should I come to you?... Yes, I'll go on looking for you, as if you were still alive. Now I remember what you look like. Goodbye... (*He tries to leave, but his coat is caught on the railings round the grave.*) Are you holding on to me? Is there something else you want to say to me? (*He listens and smiles gently.*) No, I'll never forget you again... Why are you laughing?

(*DON JUAN pulls free, terrified, and clutches at his heart. The MAID returns.*)

MAID: It's getting very dark, are you going to stay on?

DON JUAN: (*Looking up at the sky.*) It's snowing...

MAID: (*Smiles.*) You look like a real snowman already...

DON JUAN: (*Looks up and smiles gently.*) Yes, it's getting warmer all the time...

(*DON JUAN sits down on a stone.*)

MAID: (*Frightened.*) Are you all right?

DON JUAN: The snowman is tired.

(*Silence.*)

MAID: On that cold stone, you'll catch your death. Do you mind if I go now, I've still got half the laundry...

DON JUAN: (*Dully.*) Please do...please do.

MAID: Can you find your own way back?

(*DON JUAN looks round again, as if he were being followed.*)

DON JUAN: I'm waiting for someone.

MAID: Then I'll be on my way, sir! But don't wait too long!

(*The MAID exits. DON JUAN, alone, speaks again to his dead bride.*)

DON JUAN: Will it be long?... You can laugh if you like, you can laugh... What harm's the snowman done to you? (*He smiles gently.*) Never mind, hit him, he'll be gone tomorrow anyway... It's getting warmer all the time... Goodbye, snowman...

The End.

FIGARO GETS DIVORCED

for Louise

Preface

The comedy *Figaro Gets a Divorce* begins some years after Beaumarchais' *The Marriage of Figaro*. Nevertheless I have taken the liberty of setting the play in our own time because the problems of revolution are first: timeless, and second: especially topical in our time. It is not the great French Revolution of 1789 that is meant here but quite simply any revolution, since every powerful upheaval has the same common denominator in its relationship to that which we respect, or disdain, as humanity. In *The Marriage of Figaro* there are rumbles of the coming revolution; in *Figaro Gets a Divorce* there will probably be no rumbles, for humanity is not accompanied by any storms, it is only a weak light in the darkness. Let us hope all the same that no storm, however great, will be able to extinguish it.

Ödön von Horváth

Louise Adey, Stephen Daldry and Professor Trangott Krischke have all made invaluable contributions to this trnaslation, I owe them my deep gratitude.

IH

Characters

COUNT ALMAVIVA

THE COUNTESS
his wife

FIGARO
Valet to the Count

SUSANNE
Figaro's wife and chambermaid to the Countess

FOUR BORDER-GUARDS

OFFICER

DOCTOR

FORESTER

MIDWIFE

HEADMASTER

MAID

ANTONIO
Susanne's uncle and the castle gardener

FANCHETTE
his daughter

PEDRILLO
her husband, formerly groom to Count Almaviva

POLICEMAN

CHERUBIN
former page to Count Almaviva

GUEST

CARLOS
an orphan

MAURIZIO
another orphan

Other ORPHANS

The play is set some time after 'The Marriage of Figaro'

Figaro Gets Divorced was first performed in this translation at the Gate Theatre in 1990, with the following cast:

FIGARO, Roger Sloman

COUNT ALMAVIVA, Richard Mayes

THE COUNTESS, Ellen Sheean

SUSANNE, Diana Kent

FIRST BORDER GUARD / FORESTER / PEDRILLO, Mark Spalding

SECOND BORDER GUARD / ADALBERT, Simon Linnell

THIRD BORDER GUARD / BASIL / SERGEANT / CUSTOMER, Robin Polley

OFFICER / HEADMASTER / INSPECTOR, Peter Wear

JOSEPHA / FRAULEIN DOKTOR, Joanna Wake

MIDWIFE, Christine Drummond

ANTONIO, Brian Badcoe

FANCHETTE, Kate Paul

CHERUBIN, Paul Besterman

CAESAR, Robin Clifford

ORPHANS, Seamus Gonzalez, Chloë Sutcliffe, Carra Rodway, Katrina Manson, Oliver, Zoë and Edward Lynch Bell, Eileen Roell

Director, Stephen Daldry

Designer, Ian MacNeil

Music, Stephen Warbeck

Lighting Designer, Ace McCarron

Production Manager, Caroline Maude

ACT ONE

Scene 1

In the depths of the forest near the border. COUNT ALMAVIVA, the COUNTESS, FIGARO and SUSANNE are fleeing from the Revolution. Only their voices can be heard as it is a pitch-black night.

COUNTESS: Where are you?

COUNT: Over here.

COUNTESS: I can't see anything.

COUNT: This is the blackest night of my life.

(*SUSANNE lets out a scream.*)

FIGARO: What's the matter?

SUSANNE: I just stepped in something soft.

COUNTESS: I hope there aren't any snakes round here.

SUSANNE: God help us!

(*A pale moon breaks through the clouds and now the fugitives become visible.*)

COUNT: (*Looking heavenward; ironically.*) The moon is waxing.

COUNTESS: (*Looking round.*) Do snakes bite at night too?

(*SUSANNE shudders with fright.*)

FIGARO: My dear lady – gracious Countess – if I may most humbly make a request. Please don't confuse the situation any further. It's already confused enough without snakes.

COUNT: Amen to that!

SUSANNE: I'm covered in scratches from the undergrowth.

COUNTESS: And my clothes are all torn –

(*In the distance a shot is heard.*)

SUSANNE: (*Anxiously.*) What was that?

FIGARO: A shot. But we are safe.

COUNTESS: I must sit down. (*She sits down on a tree-root.*)

COUNT: (*Talking slowly and softly to FIGARO.*) Are we definitely over the border now?

FIGARO: Count, I know every clearing here. To the left is the lake, to the right the gorge, over yonder the moor and behind us our own dear fatherland.

COUNT: Let's hope you're right. For the last twenty-four hours I've been wondering what crime I committed that made it necessary for me to sneak out of the land of my fathers like a common criminal, just in order to save my skin.

FIGARO: You are the honourable Count, Your Honour, highest noble lord by birth, judge and master of all you survey. Are those not crimes enough? (*He smiles ambiguously.*)

COUNT: The events of the last few days are unbelievable. His Majesty murdered, the nobility driven out and killed, estates plundered and churches destroyed, castles looted – a baker's boy is Field Marshal, a cobbler is President and a clerk is our ambassador in London! Privileges abolished, equal rights for all, whether prince or vagrant: equal rights. No, this is all wrong and things can't go on like this, it just flies in the face of the divine law. No one would ever have dreamt of such a thing happening.

FIGARO: Apart from those who brought about the revolution.

(*The COUNT stares at him wide-eyed.*)

COUNTESS: (*Anxiously.*) There's somebody there –

SUSANNE: Where?

(*They all listen.*)

COUNTESS: (*Without expression.*) We're being hunted.

FIGARO: There's nobody there.

COUNT: You can always hear footsteps in the forest at night.

SUSANNE: Especially in autumn when the leaves are falling.

(*Silence.*)

COUNT: (*Tenderly to the COUNTESS.*) We must move on, my dear –

COUNTESS: (*Softly.*) I'd like to go to sleep.

COUNT: Here? In the forest?

(*The COUNTESS looks at him with wide eyes and hums a melancholy air. The COUNT puts his hand over his eyes.*)

FIGARO: (*In an attempt to cheer her up.*) Gracious Countess, I once spoke with a man given up for dead and he said he'd rather be a hunted animal in the undergrowth than an emperor under the ground. Better alive but in bed than in heaven and dead. Gracious Countess, I swear to you that we'll reach the first village in half an hour at the latest – I can feel it in my bones. Rely on me and my infamous instinct!

COUNTESS: (*Who cannot help smiling slightly.*) Your instinct, my dear fellow, with all due respect –

SUSANNE: (*Interrupting her, also in an attempt to cheer her up.*) Oh yes, your Grace! I won't hear a word against Figaro's instincts! Everything that he prophesies comes about and he has prophesied everything.

COUNT: Even the Revolution?

FIGARO: Prophesying that wouldn't exactly have required genius.

COUNT: No genius required?

FIGARO: (*Evasively.*) We were all deaf. Or blind.

SUSANNE: I can see a light! Over there!

(*They all look.*)

COUNT: I can't see anything.

COUNTESS: Where's my lorgnette?

FIGARO: Yes, it's a light all right. I can see it clearly – without doubt it's a house, gracious Countess!

COUNTESS: God help us! (*She stands up.*) I do believe I'm in hell and hell is just one great forest of trees.

Scene 2

It is four hours later and still night. At a border post one and a half miles away from the Revolution. An official-looking room with a desk, cupboard, iron bedstead etc. Four GUARDS are on night-duty. The FIRST is sitting at the desk and reading the newspaper; he is the oldest. The SECOND is playing chess with the THIRD and the FOURTH is lying on the bed idly smoking a cigarette.

FIRST GUARD: We're getting reinforcements. (*He reads.*)
'As a result of the bloody confusion in our neighbouring
kingdom the Royal Ministry of War has, in agreement
with the Royal Ministry of the Interior, taken the
decision to strengthen the border posts by deploying the
army. These measures are designed on the one hand to
prevent the influx of undesirable elements and on the
other to prevent the spread of heretical revolutionary
doctrines' – (*He looks up from the paper.*) – 'To prevent'
that's very good, I'm sure, but you can't hold up the
inevitable march of progress in the course of world
history, I fear – (*He grins.*)

SECOND GUARD: Check!
(*The THIRD GUARD captures a piece.*)
Damn, I've overlooked the king!

THIRD GUARD: If you overlook the king you've
overlooked everything –

FIRST GUARD: I was just reading a highly interesting
eye-witness account of how the king was assassinated –
(*He reads.*) 'He died like a king' – what crap! How else is
a king supposed to die, if not like a king, if he *is* a king!
(*He looks round, waiting for agreement, but none is
forthcoming.*)

THIRD GUARD: Check!

FOURTH GUARD: (*Suddenly to the FIRST.*) D'you know
Kitty?

FIRST GUARD: (*Confused.*) Who's Kitty?

FOURTH GUARD: If you don't know her then it's not of
any interest. She's a barmaid at the Wild Boar.

FIRST GUARD: (*Flaring up.*) Spare me that, you bastard!
(*Silence.*)

FOURTH GUARD: Kitty's got the longest legs in the
world.

SECOND GUARD: And the longest lips. They flap.

THIRD GUARD: Mate.

SECOND GUARD: (*Jumping up.*) Damn it!

FIRST GUARD: I really don't understand you lot any
more, comrades! Only a mile and a half from here a new

world order is being born; earth-shattering events are sweeping away the centuries like a hurricane and here you are playing chess and rabbiting on about a barmaid's lips!

(*The OFFICER enters. The FOUR GUARDS jump to attention and salute. The OFFICER takes off his coat and gloves, sits down at the desk.*)

OFFICER: Anything new to report?

FIRST GUARD: Beg to report, sir, everything under control.

OFFICER: (*Signing forms.*) Has the rabble over there been shooting in this direction again?

FIRST GUARD: Beg to report, sir, only joyful shots fired in the air.

OFFICER: Their kind of joy usually brings corpses. Cannibals! Anything else to report?

FIRST GUARD: Beg to report, one arrest, sir. Four people, sir.

(*The OFFICER looks up in surprise.*)

SECOND GUARD: I was on my rounds, sir, and I came across the aforesaid persons not far from the gorge.

OFFICER: Fugitives?

SECOND GUARD: It would appear so, sir. They had got lost and were going round in a circle. The older woman was exhausted.

THIRD GUARD: She was done for –

SECOND GUARD: They had no papers on them.

FIRST GUARD: And as the man behaved in a very obstreperous manner when we arrested them we took it upon ourselves to find these pearls during a search of the allegedly exhausted prisoner –

(*He hands over a small box to the OFFICER.*)

OFFICER: (*Opening it.*) Well, well, well. (*He looks at the pearl necklace.*) If these aren't fakes then our prisoners are real aristocrats.

SECOND GUARD: Or common criminals.

THIRD GUARD: Without any papers it's hard to tell the difference.

(*The FIRST GUARD gives a laugh.*)

OFFICER: (*Pricking up his ears.*) What's that supposed to mean?
(*FIRST GUARD stands to attention.*)
(*Fixing him with his gaze he suddenly yells.*) Silence! (*To the FIRST GUARD, almost quietly.*) Bring them in. All four of them.
FIRST GUARD: Yessir! (*Exits to the cells.*)
OFFICER: Which one of you knows Kitty?
FOURTH GUARD: Beg to request, sir, who's Kitty?
OFFICER: Kitty is going to have a baby. She claims that a border guard is the father but she doesn't know which one. Be very careful, gentlemen! This matter must be cleared up. (*He points to the SECOND and THIRD GUARDS.*) You or you. (*He points to the FOURTH.*) Or you.
(*The FIRST GUARD returns with the COUNT and FIGARO.*)
(*To the FIRST GUARD.*) And the two women?
COUNT: My wife has collapsed.
OFFICER: (*Stops short and looks round rather helplessly.*) Hmm. (*To the FIRST.*) And the other one?
FIGARO: (*Forestalling the FIRST GUARD.*) The other one has stayed in the cell in order to look after Her Grace, the sick Countess.
OFFICER: (*Stopping short once again.*) Countess?
FIRST GUARD: Beg to report, sir, it seems to me that she's not putting it on, sir. She's lying on the ground unable to move.
OFFICER: Call a doctor.
FIRST GUARD: (*Off.*) Yessir!
COUNT: (*Ironically to the OFFICER.*) I thank you, sir.
OFFICER: (*To the COUNT.*) Step forward.
(*The COUNT does so.*)
Your name?
COUNT: Count Almaviva.
OFFICER: Profession?
COUNT: Knight Commander in the diplomatic service of my unfortunate King. Ambassador in London, Lisbon and Rome.

OFFICER: Please sit down.

(*The COUNT doesn't move. The OFFICER points to a chair.*)
Please –

COUNT: (*Remains standing.*) I protest. As I emerge from Hell, thanking Heaven for my escape, I find myself treated like a criminal.

OFFICER: Since you have crossed over our hermetically sealed border with neither papers nor permits it is my duty to undertake an official investigation. Should it turn out that this illegal crossing of the border is merely an act of self-protection then you will have nothing to fear.

COUNT: I would have been killed.

OFFICER: You don't have to convince me.

COUNT: It's the law of the jungle over there.

OFFICER: Cannibals.

COUNT: (*Bowing stiffly.*) And as far as my authorization papers are concerned I would ask you to bear in mind that I have the honour and pleasure to count your Under-Secretary of State as one of my few friends. I know him from my time in London where he was then Commercial Attaché. He will be happy to vouch for my identity at any time.

OFFICER: I'll give you an opportunity first thing in the morning to communicate with the Under-Secretary of State. And I'll see to it that your lady wife is taken to hospital as soon as the doctor has examined her. Now would you like to sit down? (*He smiles courteously.*)

COUNT: Will you allow me to go to my wife?

OFFICER: Whenever you wish, my dear Count.

(*The COUNT bows stiffly and goes off to the cells.*)

OFFICER: (*To FIGARO.*) Step forward. Your name?

FIGARO: Figaro.

OFFICER: Profession?

FIGARO: Valet to the noble and honourable Count Almaviva.

OFFICER: Date of birth?

FIGARO: Unknown.

OFFICER: What does that mean?

FIGARO: I am an orphan.

OFFICER: And your approximate age?

FIGARO: No idea.

OFFICER: Absolute nonsense! You must be able to remember various significant dates in your life from which you can reconstruct your age!

FIGARO: If I were to reconstruct my age from the various significant dates in my life then I would erroneously conclude that I am approximately three hundred years old – since I have so many significant dates to my credit. Stolen by gypsies before I've any idea who my parents are; I run away from them because I don't want to be a vagabond; I look, I search, I struggle to find an honest profession, only to find all paths blocked and all doors closed to me. I was starving hungry and in debt – what a wonderful fate! Finally I found an open door and went after every conceivable profession just so as to survive; I was a journalist, a waiter, a politician, a gambler, a travelling salesman, a barber; at times I was the master, at times the servant, depending on the whim of fate; ambitious through vanity, industrious through necessity but sluggish by nature and inclination. A flatterer on occasion, a poet for relaxation, a musician when required, a lover as the fancy takes me. I've seen, done, delighted in everything, had no illusions; I was only too alert and awake until one day – I married! That was the milestone in my life, the great moment of reflection and renewal. Since the marriage of that Figaro I have been a different man –

OFFICER: (*Interrupting him, utterly amazed by his sudden loquacity. He strikes his fist on the table.*) That's enough! (*To the GUARDS.*) Has he been drinking?

FIGARO: Yes.

OFFICER: (*Harshly.*) I can see that.

FIGARO: Since I haven't had anything to eat for the past twenty-four hours and since neither my wife nor the Count nor the Countess were particularly interested in the little drop of schnapps that we had with us, I swigged that little drop at the moment of our arrest in order to protect it from imminent confiscation.

OFFICER: (*Sighing in desperation.*) A court-jester! (*To FIGARO.*) Wife's name?

FIGARO: Susanne. She is Lady's maid to Her Grace the Countess.

OFFICER: Aha.

FIGARO: We have been married for six years.

OFFICER: That's of no interest to me.

(*The FIRST GUARD returns with the DOCTOR.*)

DOCTOR: (*Greeting the OFFICER.*) Has someone died?

FIGARO: Not yet.

OFFICER: (*Smiling involuntarily.*) Just a sick woman. Please follow me – (*Exits to the cells with the DOCTOR.*)

FIGARO: Would one of you gentlemen happen to have a cigarette on you?

FIRST GUARD: Smoking's forbidden!

SECOND GUARD: Come off it, he's not a murderer! (*To FIGARO.*) Catch, court-jester! (*He throws him a cigarette.*)

FIGARO: (*Catching it.*) Thanks, general. (*He lights it.*)

SECOND GUARD: (*To the FIRST.*) He's just glad to be alive.

(*Silence.*)

THIRD GUARD: (*To FIGARO.*) Are things really as chaotic in your country as our newspapers make out?

FIGARO: It's not that bad, they're just setting fire to everything and killing off the ruling classes.

FIRST GUARD: There you are! I knew all along these horror stories were exaggerated!

SECOND GUARD: (*To FIGARO.*) Is it true that all border-guards have been dismissed? And without a pension?

FIGARO: Just more horror-stories! The worthy border-guards are carrying out their duties as if nothing had happened.

FIRST GUARD: There you are!

FOURTH GUARD: And what about maintenance payments? I read that they've introduced free love and women are now common property – but what I'd like to know is who looks after the kiddies?

FIGARO: According to the revolutionary manifesto: the general public.

SECOND GUARD: Damn it! We could do with a bit of that!

FOURTH GUARD: (*Grinning.*) That'd be a manifesto –

FIRST GUARD: A political act of benefit to the population!

FIGARO: According to the manifesto the whole business of relations between the sexes is to be fully revised. Take me for instance: I've often argued with my wife about having children because I was always against it. A valet, and a lady's maid, I argued, couldn't allow themselves the luxury of having children. The first and fifteenth of each month they could be dismissed and it'd be an act of criminal irresponsibility as long as your very livelihood depends on the whim of your lord and master.

FIRST GUARD: (*To the other GUARDS.*) There you are again! The whim of the lord and master and meanwhile this good man – (*Pointing to FIGARO.*) God knows why, stands here suspected of being an emissary of the revolution. On the contrary he hates it and fled from it –

FIGARO: (*Interrupting him.*) Excuse me but I don't hate the revolution. Why on earth should I do that? I find it entirely understandable that anyone should rebel; I know from intimate experience that the rulers who've just been driven out have a long criminal record, and I felt in my bones that there was an explosion coming – I heard the rumbling in the distance and I prophesied it.

THIRD GUARD: So you flirted with the revolution, did you?

FIGARO: I never flirt. Gentlemen, I was the first servant to tell his master the truth.

(*Silence.*)

FIRST GUARD: If you told the truth, why then did you not stay at home in your own country?

FIGARO: There are highly personal reasons for that. Gentlemen, when I discussed it with my wife, whether we should stay or flee with our masters, she said that there was such a thing as loyalty and that we don't only have duties to ourselves but also towards our fellow human beings, even if it's only our own masters. We'd lived with them through the good old days, she said, and we should stay with them now in their hour of misfortune too – you see, my wife really has her heart in the right place.

FOURTH GUARD: So in fact you only fled because of your wife.

FIGARO: (*Stops short, hesitates; then quietly.*) Perhaps. (*He ponders. Silence.*)

SECOND GUARD: I often wonder why there are actually two different kinds of human being, man and woman –

THIRD GUARD: God's the man to ask about that.

SECOND GUARD: There ain't no God to ask.

FIGARO: Could I please speak to my wife?

FOURTH GUARD: Any time you like.

FIGARO: Thank you.
(*He is about to go off to the cells when he meets SUSANNE in the doorway; she is just coming out.*)

SUSANNE: Ah, there you are –

FIGARO: I was just about to come and find you.

SUSANNE: (*Smiling.*) Funny. I've been thinking about you for the last five minutes.

FIGARO: And I've been thinking about you. Must be telepathy – (*He gives a grin.*)

SUSANNE: Where were you all this time?

FIGARO: I've been talking to these gentlemen here.

SUSANNE: (*Smiling.*) I was beginning to think you'd walked out on me –

FIGARO: No. How is the Countess?

SUSANNE: Not well.

FIGARO: What's the doctor have to say?

SUSANNE: He hasn't said anything.
(*Silence.*)

FIGARO: She'll get better.

SUSANNE: I don't know how you can be so indifferent –

FIGARO: It's just that I'm feeling rather nervous.

SUSANNE: The poor Countess can't relax at all; now she's had an injection but she keeps hearing footsteps and she's convinced she's being hunted –

FIRST GUARD: (*Sighing.*) Nobody is hunting her here! In this country we have law and order.

SUSANNE: Thank God for that! I'm just happy to be over the border; all hell's been let loose over there! You can't imagine it, gentlemen, not in your wildest dreams! Nothing but crimes, robbery, murder and –

FIGARO: (*Interrupting.*) Come on now! Don't exaggerate so!

SUSANNE: (*Puzzled.*) Exaggerate? Me!

FIGARO: What's happening always happens when there's a revolution and it's perfectly logical since from a revolutionary standpoint the people are in the right.

SUSANNE: Right?

FIGARO: There are two kinds of right. Like this or like that. Take you and me for instance, nobody would've touched a hair of our heads if we'd just stayed quietly at home, like all your relations did, Antonio, Pedrillo, Fanchette – no one would've killed us; I might possibly even have become warden of the castle –

SUSANNE: (*Cutting in on him.*) Castle warden?!

FIGARO: Why not?
(*Silence.*)

SUSANNE: (*Staring at him.*) I've never heard you talk like that –

FIGARO: (*Gazing intently at her.*) No? Have you forgotten?
(*Silence.*)

SUSANNE: (*Looks round almost in fright; softly.*) I must go back to the Countess now. (*Off to the cells.*)
(*Silence.*)

FIRST GUARD: (*To FIGARO.*) Tell me, honoured sir; how come your good lady wife reacts so differently from you to such earth-shattering events?

FIGARO: (*Grinning.*) She still has her faith in God.

Scene 3*

A few days later in a foreign capital. A small but exclusive Jeweller's shop. A concealed door leads to the JEWELLER's private office. He is an elegant young man with glasses. He is standing in the doorway and talking to his ASSISTANT. It is morning and the sun is shining.

ASSISTANT: You really must see this film, sir, it's a unique historical document. You see it all in detail, his head and the revolver – bang! He's dead. Fantastic!

JEWELLER: Incredible.

ASSISTANT: Go and see it today, they say it's going to be banned because people applauded yesterday. It's not every day you see the assassination of a king live.

JEWELLER: When does the performance start?

ASSISTANT: The last one begins at ten.

JEWELLER: Get me two tickets, I'll take Fräulein Mia to it. (*Exits into his private office.*)

ASSISTANT: (*Telephoning.*) Hello! Yes, two tickets for the last performance in the name of Tenbroeck, the jeweller. Only boxes left? Fine. Hello, it is still the assassination that's on, isn't it? It is still on, that's alright then. Goodbye. (*He hangs up.*)
(*COUNT enters with FIGARO.*)
Can I help you?

COUNT: May I speak to the jeweller, Herr Tenbroeck?

ASSISTANT: Who shall I say it is?

COUNT: Count Almaviva.

ASSISTANT: At once. Your Grace! (*Exits through the concealed door.*)

COUNT: (*Watching him go.*) I remember that concealed door very clearly. This is where I bought the ring that the Countess lost last summer – d'you remember?

FIGARO: I remember it very clearly.

COUNT: It was my honeymoon, but here nothing has changed. A conservative establishment.

FIGARO: You can tell by the smell.

COUNT: (*Smiling.*) Yes.

* This scene was omitted from the London premiere

93

JEWELLER: (*Comes out of the door, followed by his ASSISTANT.*) How can I help Your Grace?

COUNT: I'd like to speak to Herr Tenbroeck, the jeweller.

JEWELLER: I am Herr Tenbroeck.

COUNT: You? I apologise but I had a very different image of you, with a white beard – (*He smiles.*)

JEWELLER: (*Without smiling.*) That was my Papa.

COUNT: Ah, yes!

JEWELLER: And when did you meet Papa?

COUNT: Oh, it's been an eternity –

JEWELLER: That's why. He's been dead these last eighteen years.

COUNT: Dead? (*Looking round.*) But everything's just as it used to be – apart from that –

JEWELLER: Yes, unfortunately everything is rather antiquated. Next month I'm having a radical reorganization.

COUNT: Really?

(*Silence.*)

JEWELLER: To what do I owe the honour, Your Grace?

COUNT: Do you know who I am?

JEWELLER: To be perfectly honest, the name is familiar to me but for the moment I can't quite place –

COUNT: (*Interrupting him.*) I'm an émigré.

(*JEWELLER becomes increasingly more reticent.*)

Yes, the last few days were not without their ups and downs. My poor wife has fallen very ill as a result of our untimely flight, she's in the Park Sanatorium suffering from a serious nervous collapse.

JEWELLER: (*Indifferently.*) How terrible.

COUNT: She'll have to stay there for three weeks and then we shall go to the mountains. The healthy atmosphere up there.

JEWELLER: I really envy you that. I'm a dedicated winter sports enthusiast.

COUNT: (*Interrupting him.*) Forgive me, but we'll be back home again for the winter sports. The present state of affairs in my unhappy fatherland cannot continue. It's a revolt by the most barbaric elements – and therefore an event which is bad by definition. It will and must be crushed by the healthy mentality of our people, above all that of the peasants.

JEWELLER: (*Smiling indifferently.*) Let's hope so.

COUNT: It'll all be over in two months at most.

JEWELLER: (*Exchanging glances with his ASSISTANT.*) And in what way can I be of service?

COUNT: (*Becoming slightly embarrassed.*) It's rather a delicate matter –

JEWELLER: Of course! (*Goes off with the COUNT through the concealed door.*)

(*Silence.*)

ASSISTANT: Are you an émigré as well?

FIGARO: Yes.

ASSISTANT: D'you know Prince Bisamsky?

FIGARO: The fat one or the tall one who's a bit dim?

ASSISTANT: I only know the fat one.

FIGARO: He's dim too.

ASSISTANT: He came in here with a diadem yesterday but we didn't purchase.

(*FIGARO pricks up his ears.*)

Every other émigré brings us at least one diadem, we're swamped with the bloody things.

FIGARO: You don't say!

ASSISTANT: Your country's aristocracy used to provide us with our best customers.

FIGARO: That's all over now.

ASSISTANT: (*Pompously.*) That's how it is. Instead of buying they now make competition for us by selling into the bargain. Prices have really gone through the floor, the market's flooded with diamonds –

FIGARO: (*Interrupting him.*) Pearls too?

ASSISTANT: Pearls are a nuisance!

FIGARO: That is good news.

ASSISTANT: (*Glancing at the concealed door.*) Don't think he'll have much joy. The wheels of history won't stop for him, let alone go into reverse. Everything over in two months, what a joke! Eh?

FIGARO: (*Grins grimly.*) I don't answer questions like that.

ASSISTANT: It'll last for a thousand years.

FIGARO: Then it's hardly going to make any odds to me.

JEWELLER: (*Returning from his private office with the COUNT.*) I'll have a contract drawn up for you! (*Under his breath.*) We've really hit the jackpot with this one – (*To the COUNT.*) Just a minute, Your Grace. (*Goes off through the concealed door with his ASSISTANT.*)

COUNT: (*Watching the JEWELLER.*) Swindling bastard.

FIGARO: If I understand correctly the swindling bastard has just bought the pearls?

COUNT: (*Smiling.*) Yes, but at a sixth of the price we'd hoped for –

FIGARO: (*Dismayed.*) Only a sixth?

COUNT: What's it matter? I don't know how to haggle, all I can do is buy.

FIGARO: Your Grace really should have let me do the haggling –

COUNT: What's done is done and we haven't lost the necklace yet. The Countess'll be wearing it again soon, very soon in fact!

FIGARO: Touch wood!

COUNT: I'm just glad that we are rid of these wretched financial worries of the past few days. Now we can start to live properly again.

FIGARO: We could live off a sixth for three years anyway.

COUNT: (*Interrupting him.*) Three years! Are you crazy? Am I supposed to move into furnished rooms in some middle-class boarding-house perhaps? An Almaviva will continue to live in the style to which he is accustomed, allowing himself all the luxuries to which his birth has entitled him. For him emigration shall simply be a pleasure trip and the rabble should take cognizance of the fact that it isn't going to bother me. This shopkeeper – (*Pointing at the concealed door.*) – is drivelling on about five hundred years.

FIGARO: Only five hundred?

COUNT: (*Who's not listening to him.*) How short-sighted the world is! No, I can see the future quite clearly, we'll be

home before the first snows and meanwhile I shall be
doing my utmost to shorten the time, I'll spare no pains
to set everything in motion to resolve the situation –
Don't forget to remind me that my friend, the
Under-Secretary of State, is expecting me tomorrow. At
two-thirty at the Ministry.

FIGARO: (*Horrified.*) Ministry? Dear Lord!

COUNT: (*Surprised.*) What's the matter?

FIGARO: Forgive me, but I completely forgot to give Your
Grace this letter which was handed in this morning – (*He
takes the letter out of his pocket and hands it over to the
COUNT.*) It's from the Ministry. Forgive me!

COUNT: (*Opens the letter, reads it and stops short; he then
hands it back to FIGARO and says quietly.*) Read it.

FIGARO: (*Reading.*) Hmm.

(*Silence.*)

COUNT: And what do you say to that?

FIGARO: It's what I expected.

COUNT: A lot of fine words for a piece of cowardice I
shouldn't visit my 'friend' in the Ministry because the
appearance of a prominent émigré might arouse
suspicion that the trade agreement is not entirely to be
trusted – Hmm – (*He smiles.*) Fine, then I'll write articles
about ominous trade agreements with Barbarians, one
article after another, I've got the evidence to hand and
I'll prepare for battle.

FIGARO: I fear no one will print those articles.

COUNT: Then I'll make public speeches.

FIGARO: They'll be forbidden.

COUNT: (*Pricking up his ears.*) You think so?

FIGARO: Or else Your Grace simply won't have an
audience.

COUNT: (*Staring at him.*) And why not?

FIGARO: Because no one wants to fall out with the
Barbarians, partly because they sympathise and partly
because they're frightened.

(*Silence.*)

JEWELLER: (*Coming out of his office holding a document and
followed by his ASSISTANT.*) The contract, Your Grace!

Scene 4

Three months later. High up in the mountains, in one of the loveliest health resorts in the world. A wide hotel-terrace belonging to COUNT ALMAVIVA's apartment with a magnificent view out over the Alpine peaks. On a skating-rink in front of the hotel music is playing. SUSANNE is helping the COUNTESS, who is now fully recovered, to put on her skates. Snow and sunshine.

COUNTESS: I'd never have dreamed, even a few weeks ago, that I'd ever go on the ice again –

SUSANNE: All bad things come to an end, Countess. The skates fit perfectly.

COUNTESS: They're too tight for me.

SUSANNE: That'll pass!

FIGARO: (*Entering.*) The skating teacher is waiting, gracious Countess.

COUNTESS: I'm ready. Where on earth is the Count?

FIGARO: His Grace the Count is in the casino.

COUNTESS: (*Smiling.*) He'd do better to practise some sport rather than gambling since he always loses.

SUSANNE: Enjoy yourself, Countess.

COUNTESS: Lie down and enjoy the sun, Susanne! (*Exits.*)

SUSANNE: Come on, Figaro, let's make ourselves comfortable – (*Moving two deckchairs into the sun.*) D'you know how high up we are here? Two thousand metres above sea-level.

FIGARO: Still too low for the height of the prices. This is the most expensive winter health resort in the world. And the most expensive hotel.

SUSANNE: But you and I aren't paying for it.

FIGARO: You think not?

SUSANNE: (*Offering him a seat.*) Would His Grace like to –

FIGARO: The sun up at this height is unhealthy. It's only healthy for sick people.

SUSANNE: Who says so?

FIGARO: I do.

SUSANNE: (*Smiling.*) Scared of getting ill? Poor Figaro!

FIGARO: Mock me if you like.

SUSANNE: Oh Figaro, how you have changed! What's the matter with you? We've been away three months now, first the poor Countess was in the sanatorium for seven weeks –

FIGARO: (*Interrupting her.*) That was no sanatorium, that was a lunatic asylum for the upper classes. The most expensive lunatic asylum in the world.
(*Silence.*)

SUSANNE: You used not to be so pedantic.

FIGARO: I've got my worries.

SUSANNE: You make worries for yourself! We never had it so good before the exile. Grand hotels all the time and we're treated like guests.

FIGARO: Like paying guests. How long can we afford this luxurious life-style our masters are indulging in? Till Easter, and what then? Then there won't be any more pearls to cast before the swine like we've done up till now!

SUSANNE: (*Smearing white sun-cream on her face.*) Yesterday evening the Count said to the Countess that we'd be back home in four weeks at the latest.

FIGARO: (*Leaping up.*) I can't listen to any more of this drivel! Three months ago he said it'd all be over in two months. Drivel! Eight weeks ago he said it'd all be over in six weeks. Drivel. Four weeks ago he said we'd be home by Christmas and Christmas is the day after tomorrow. Drivel again. I tell you it's all a load of drivel, the situation's stabilising and everyone's capitulating and we're never going to see the end of it, only the end of us! Drivel, drivel and more drivel!

SUSANNE: The count is a shrewd diplomat, d'you think you know any better than he does?

FIGARO: (*Stops abruptly and gazes at her.*) Choose between him and me.

SUSANNE: (*Puzzled.*) What's that mean?

FIGARO: Susanne, a world order has collapsed. When we crossed the forest that night in the middle of the wood I told the Countess all that nonsense about the man given up for dead in order to give her courage – d'you remember? Well it suddenly became clear to me that I talk to those given up for dead and that I tell lies when I play the court-jester in order to plead for my life to the dead and dying. It would have been better for the Count and Countess if they'd never crossed the border, if they'd stayed and been murdered –

SUSANNE: (*Horrified.*) Figaro!

FIGARO: A world order has collapsed, an old world order. The Count and Countess are no longer alive, they just haven't realised it yet. They are laid out on their biers in the Grand Hotel thinking the undertakers are porters, the grave-diggers head-waiters and the layer-out a masseuse. They change their underwear daily but it still remains a shroud, they perfume themselves but they always smell of flowers rotting on a tombstone. They're heading for the grave, Susanne! Is that where you want to go too? I don't.

SUSANNE: (*Anxiously.*) I don't understand you, Figaro.

FIGARO: We must separate from the Almavivas.

SUSANNE: Separate?

FIGARO: We must make ourselves independent. Today is the first of the month.

SUSANNE: Are you mad?

FIGARO: I am no shrewd diplomat it is true, but I do know what I want. (*He pulls a newspaper out of his pocket.*) I read here in the small ads: there is a barber's shop for sale.

SUSANNE: Barber's shop?

FIGARO: Yes, I'm going to be a barber again. (*He reads a small ad.*) 'High-class hairdressing salon for sale as result of marriage. In Grosshadersdorf.' Grosshadersdorf is an upwardly mobile, medium-sized village with three thousand four hundred inhabitants. Beautiful surroundings, hilly landscape. I've made enquiries. Plenty of woodland.

(*Silence.*)

SUSANNE: (*Staring at him.*) Do you mean it seriously?

FIGARO: Absolutely. To pay us off the Count only has to give us the amount that it costs the four of us to stay

here a week, not counting of course the massive sums
that he gambles away each day in the casino. No,
Susanne, I'm not going along with it any more, we're
going to escape and make ourselves independent. What
are you staring at me like that for?

SUSANNE: Because something's just occurred to me.

FIGARO: What's that?

SUSANNE: You won't like it.

FIGARO: You can tell me anything.

(*Silence.*)

SUSANNE: When we got married you always said that two
people who were as dependent on their employers as a
chambermaid and a valet couldn't afford the luxury of
having children, and I could see what you meant –

FIGARO: There you are then!

SUSANNE: But you also always said that if one day we
became our own masters then at once – 'at once' you
said.

FIGARO: That's right. But first I must see which way the
game's going.

SUSANNE: What game d'you mean?

FIGARO: The waiting game, to see whether we remain our
own masters.

SUSANNE: (*Smiling oddly.*) How timorous you've become –

FIGARO: I'm not a coward, I just respect the future!

(*Silence.*)

SUSANNE: (*Suddenly.*) The Count'll look after me all right.

FIGARO: Nobody has to look after you except me!

SUSANNE: I'm staying.

FIGARO: Oh yes? You intend to leave me when it was only
because of you that I fled in the first place?

SUSANNE: That's not true, you would have done it out of
loyalty to the Count anyway –

FIGARO: (*Interrupting her.*) That's possible, but I'd also
have stayed behind if you'd stayed! When it comes down
to it I emigrated solely and exclusively because of you, I
emigrated for reasons of marital fidelity, nothing else!

(*Silence.*)

COUNT: (*Coming up to SUSANNE.*) Where's the Countess?

FIGARO: Skating on thin ice.

(*The COUNT looks at FIGARO in surprise and eyes him suspiciously for he detects a certain lack of respect in his tone.*)

SUSANNE: (*Trying to save the situation.*) Figaro's so edgy today –

COUNT: (*Somewhat ironic.*) Ah! That'd be the weather or have you two been arguing again?

FIGARO: No, Your Grace, we're both in agreement.

COUNT: That would of course be a welcome change.

(*He sits down.*

SUSANNE turns away in tears.

The COUNT looks at her in surprise.)

FIGARO: (*Making a real effort.*) Your Grace, you have written articles and delivered lectures against the new leadership –

COUNT: (*Interrupting him.*) There was no point, I accept that. The new leaders will bring one another down in four weeks at the latest –

FIGARO: (*Cutting in.*) And if, Your Grace, they don't bring one another down?

(*The COUNT looks furious.*)

Beg pardon.

(*Silence.*)

COUNT: Susanne once said you had the gift of prophecy. But I too can prophesy. Take care.

FIGARO: I don't understand you, Your Grace.

COUNT: A person who wants to be considered a part of my retinue should not always be telling me his opinion, even if it is the right one, he should rather lie to me, unconditionally agreeing with everything I say, since telling the truth in such times as these is frequently no more than covert criticism. And I'll deal with any covert criticism personally – (*He nods at him with a smile.*)

FIGARO: I would never have asked so casually, but unfortunately I cannot look to the future without worrying since I have my wife to worry about whether it suits her or not. It is my first duty. If I were in your position, Your Grace, I'd put my money in a flourishing coffee-house while there's still time.

COUNT: Are you ill? What sort of lascivious suggestion is that meant to be?

FIGARO: Forced on us by the crisis.

COUNT: Are you suffering from the crisis?

SUSANNE: (*Tearfully.*) Your Grace, he's gone mad, he wants to resign his post – he wants to resign!

(*She begins to sob.*)

COUNT: Resign?

(*He stares intently at FIGARO. Silence.*)

FIGARO: (*Embarrassed and unsure of himself.*) Today is the first of the month, Your Grace –

COUNT: (*Cutting in.*) Makes no difference. Anyone who doesn't want to stay with me can go whenever he wants. I accept.

FIGARO: Thank you, Your Grace.

(*Silence.*)

COUNT: (*To SUSANNE.*) Where do you want to go, then? D'you want to go back?

FIGARO: (*Forestalling SUSANNE.*) Not likely, Your Grace!

COUNT: (*To FIGARO.*) Take care! A returning émigré'll lose his head!

FIGARO: And quite right too.

COUNT: (*Puzzled.*) Right?

FIGARO: Your Grace, there are unfortunately two kinds of right. Like this or like that.

SUSANNE: (*Suddenly going for FIGARO.*) There are also two kinds of wrong! Like this or like that!

FIGARO: (*To SUSANNE.*) That's the way it goes.

(*Silence.*)

COUNT: (*To SUSANNE.*) So you don't want to return home?

SUSANNE: (*Crying.*) He wants to become a hairdresser again –

COUNT: Hairdresser again! (*He can't help smiling.*)

FIGARO: Your Grace, I'd like to go to Grosshadersdorf.

COUNT: (*Interrupting him.*) Doesn't interest me.

FIGARO: Just as you like.

(*Silence.*)

COUNT: How long have you been with me?

FIGARO: Nine years, Your Grace.

COUNT: Hmm. I'm sorry we are going our separate ways but I've been expecting it; I've felt for some time that you have been pursuing a policy of passive resistance.

FIGARO: Excuse me but that is nothing other than active self-preservation.

COUNT: That's the one thing I can't stomach: my dear Figaro, you've become a bourgeois – (*He gives a slight smile.*)

FIGARO: Your Grace, I've had to go hungry so often in my life that for me the word 'bourgeois' holds no terror.

COUNTESS: (*Returning from the ice-rink and seeing the COUNT.*) Ah, back from the casino already? Well now, and what have we lost today?

COUNT: Figaro and Susanne.

End of Act One.

ACT TWO

Scene 1

Nine months later in Grosshadersdorf. FIGARO has taken over the high-class hairdressing salon and is in the process of giving Frau JOSEPHA a permanent wave; she is the resolute wife of the pastry-cook ADALBERT. SUSANNE is lathering the beard of the HEADMASTER. On the left is a door leading to their private apartments. It's the end of September and almost evening.

HEADMASTER: (*To SUSANNE.*) But it's your husband who'll do the actual shaving?

FIGARO: My wife just does the lathering!

SUSANNE: (*Smiling.*) Does that frighten you?

HEADMASTER: To be honest the thought of a razor blade in such tender hands does give me a strange feeling –

JOSEPHA: (*Pointedly.*) Oh how gallant, Headmaster!

HEADMASTER: What is it the Romans say? Veni, vidi, vici.

SUSANNE: What's that mean?

FIGARO: I came, I saw, I conquered.

HEADMASTER: (*Expressing surprise, he says to FIGARO who is now shaving him.*) You know some Latin?

FIGARO: Only for domestic use, Headmaster. I'm entirely self-taught.

JOSEPHA: (*To SUSANNE who's doing her hair.*) Not so hard, young lady. My skull isn't a lump of dough, you know!

SUSANNE: I do apologise, Madam.

JOSEPHA: Just keep it nice and loose, otherwise you'll ruin all your husband's good work!

SUSANNE: (*Smiling somewhat pointedly.*) I wouldn't dream of it.

HEADMASTER: (*To FIGARO.*) Be careful, I've got a pimple there –

FIGARO: Already taken into account!

HEADMASTER: You're a genius.

JOSEPHA: (*Getting up and paying SUSANNE.*) You'll be coming tomorrow evening, won't you, Frau Figaro?

SUSANNE: Where to?

JOSEPHA: You don't know? The Humanitarian Society is holding its drama festival and my Irma is playing the main part and she looks so charming –

SUSANNE: My husband's bound to be there.

FIGARO: (*To JOSEPHA.*) My wife isn't feeling very well.

JOSEPHA: There's no need to get all coy about it, just because all the local dignitaries will be there! Really, we hardly see you at all, young lady – Well, goodbye! (*Exits.*)

FIGARO: (*Bowing obsequiously after her.*) Most honoured, Madam, most honoured! (*He casts a scathing glance at SUSANNE; he's now finished shaving the HEADMASTER and asks him.*) Hot or cold rub?

HEADMASTER: Eau de Cologne. And talc.

FIGARO: (*Powdering him.*) Thank you, sir.

HEADMASTER: (*Standing up and looking at his cheeks in the mirror.*) Give the devil his due: the most careful barber whose victim it's ever been my pleasure to be. That you should be living in Grosshadersdorf of all places is a puzzle to me.

FIGARO: (*Brushing him down.*) Circumstances, Headmaster, circumstances!

HEADMASTER: Any hairdressing-salon in any city in the world would have welcomed such talent with open arms!

FIGARO: Possibly. But I don't intend to be an employee any more; I prefer being my own master. Of course it means grafting day and night but one wants to have one's freedom, Headmaster.

HEADMASTER: What's left of your freedom if you have to graft all the time?

SUSANNE: Nothing.

(*Silence.*)

HEADMASTER: Hmm. Believe you me, Grosshadersdorf is unique; it is the kiss of death, this place. Well, on that note, goodbye all! (*Exits.*)

FIGARO: (*Bowing obsequiously.*) Most honoured,
Headmaster, most honoured. (*He shuts the door and
mutters to himself.*) What a fool.

SUSANNE: He's right.

FIGARO: I must have a serious word with you, Susanne.
It's high time. Nine months ago we took over this salon.
Thanks to my skill we have managed to get all the local
dignitaries, from the village priest to the midwife, to
come to us, for shaving, waving, crimping, manicuring
and I've even introduced pedicure et cetera et cetera –
but the greater skill lies not in winning over clients but
in not losing those same clients and to this end it is not
merely a question of first-class shaving, waving et cetera
et cetera, but of diplomacy, tricks of a psychological
nature, responding to the clients, being interested in their
problems, agreeing with their opinions, flattering their
vanity, sharing their cares, answering their questions,
laughing when they laugh, weeping when they weep –

SUSANNE: (*Interrupting him.*) Is that your idea of freedom?

FIGARO: Please don't confuse me. Let me finish what I
have to say. My freedom expresses itself not least in the
fact that I can be a hypocrite, and we need hypocrisy,
otherwise we'll find ourselves out on our ear one of these
days! You don't realise how serious the situation is. Not
long ago at that party in the sports centre you almost cut
the mayor's wife completely –

SUSANNE: (*Interrupting.*) She just went on and on about
her hernia, no one can put up with that.

FIGARO: A hernia here, a hernia there, you've got to put
up with it! You bear a responsibility and what's more it's
your clear duty to be present tomorrow evening at the
Humanitarian Society Drama Festival! The lady who
runs the *pâtisserie* is a first-class customer and you must
watch her daughter Irma perform!

SUSANNE: I'd rather stay at home and read a novel –

FIGARO: Your job isn't to read novels; it is your job to
watch that girl Irma!

SUSANNE: She's the ugliest girl in creation! A squinting
dwarf with dropsy.

FIGARO: Dropsy here, dropsy there! It's your job to find
this dancing abortion the most charming of creatures and
to clap until your hands are sore, understand!

SUSANNE: I loathe these petty bourgeois!

FIGARO: We live off these petty bourgeois whether you
love them or loathe them!

SUSANNE: If only they didn't stink so much when they get
together –

FIGARO: The times are past when we used to be
surrounded by ladies and gentlemen who led a perfumed
existence, those times are dead and gone. Finally buried.

SUSANNE: Don't pretend that you don't yearn for the old
days too!

FIGARO: I'm no longer in the habit of yearning, I've given
all that up. I am only in the habit of thinking, about
Today and about Tomorrow.

SUSANNE: (*Gloomily.*) I'll rot if I stay in this dump.
(*Suddenly shouting at him.*) I wasn't born to crimp some
pastry-cook's hair nor to find some dancing disaster
charming. Some of the greatest primadonnas have
listened to my criticisms. I wasn't born to drink beer in
smoky bars, I've drunk champagne before now, I wasn't
born to sit around at ladies' coffee-mornings discussing
their hernias, I was once confidante to a Countess.
(*Suddenly she breaks off and bursts into tears.*) If only we'd
stayed with the Almavivas!

FIGARO: I'd rather not know how the poor old Almavivas
are faring right now.

SUSANNE: (*Sobbing.*) Better than me, that's for sure!

FIGARO: How dare you say such a thing!

SUSANNE: Sometimes you talk just like our customers do –

FIGARO: Cut your coat according to your cloth, if you
don't want to catch a nasty cold. (*He grins.*)

SUSANNE: This place is Death.

FIGARO: It's not my fault we landed up here.

SUSANNE: (*Going for him again.*) And whose fault is it? Of
course! It's mine! Just because of me and my absurd
'loyalty' to our masters, that's why we emigrated and

brought this lot on ourselves when we could've stayed at home just like Uncle Antonio, Pedrillo and Fanchette – and perhaps you'd even have become castle warden, wouldn't you, eh? That's what I hear three times a day, isn't it?

FIGARO: That is not true. Only once have I expressed any such opinion!

SUSANNE: But I hear it even if you don't say it! I hear it when you're reading the newspaper, I hear it when you're looking out of the window, I hear you dreaming it when you're lying next to me in bed –

FIGARO: (*Ironically.*) And what else d'you hear?

SUSANNE: That things are all wrong between us, Figaro.
(*Silence.*)

FIGARO: How's that?

SUSANNE: When we split up with the Countess I told you I'd go anywhere with you because I belong to you – do you remember? I'll even follow you to Grosshadersdorf I said, because I love you, but I must be your wife too, really be your wife.

FIGARO: What's that supposed to mean? Aren't I your husband?

SUSANNE: Do you really not remember?
(*Silence.*
Dusk is beginning to fall.)

FIGARO: Oh, I see, that's what you mean – Hmm. Susanne, be rational. Who could possibly want the responsibility of bringing a child into the world nowadays –

SUSANNE: We are running a high-class hairdressing salon.

FIGARO: There's no such thing as high-class nowadays.

SUSANNE: How will it feel when we're old and there's no one there we can call our own. I shall never hear the word 'Mother' and you'll never hear the word 'Father'. Our whole lives will have been without any purpose.

FIGARO: Life doesn't have much purpose anyway. And how d'you know we'll grow old at all in such troubled times?

SUSANNE: When you talk like that I feel as though I'd rather be dead.

FIGARO: (*Tenderly.*) Believe me when I say I'm very fond of you.

SUSANNE: That isn't enough for me.

FIGARO: Isn't enough for you?

(*He takes off his barber's coat and puts his hat on.*)

SUSANNE: Where are you going?

FIGARO: My singing circle. Shut up shop, would you, it's past closing time and one of those local police is particularly petty-minded! (*Exits.*)

Scene 2

In a large foreign city. A cheap furnished room. The COUNTESS is sitting in the only armchair, reading short stories from the lending library. Her hair has turned white. The COUNT is standing at the window. It is snowing.

COUNT: It's snowing.

COUNTESS: (*With a smile.*) Soon be winter again. Let's hope it's a mild one with wood the price it is.

COUNT: Has the post been yet?

COUNTESS: Are you expecting something?

COUNT: Yes. A reply from the editor.

COUNTESS: It's about time.

COUNT: And we will be able to pay today.

COUNTESS: I get really scared whenever there's a knock at the door; we haven't paid a bill for a fortnight –

COUNT: An Almaviva always settles his debts.

(*There is a knock at the door.*)

Come in!

MAID: (*Bringing in two letters.*) The post, Your Grace.

(*Exits.*)

COUNT: One for you. And one from the editor –

(*He opens his letter and glances at the contents.*)

COUNTESS: (*Opens her letter and looks at the signature.*) Well I never! (*She becomes engrossed in the contents.*)

COUNT: (*Has just finished reading his letter and puts it in his pocket apathetically; in a flat voice.*) Who's written to you?

COUNTESS: Susanne.

COUNT: Susanne? I expressly requested you not to correspond with them.

COUNTESS: I'm not corresponding with them, look at the envelope. It went to the Esplanade and was sent on here.

COUNT: (*Reading the addresses on the envelope.*) Esplanade, Carlton, Regina –

COUNTESS: (*Smiling.*) Stations of the Cross.

COUNT: Steps down the ladder.

(*Silence.*)

COUNTESS: D'you still have a yearning for the Esplanade?

COUNT: (*Still staring at the addresses.*) Third floor. Furnished rooms. Frau Therese Bader's boarding-house. (*He puts the envelope on the table.*)

COUNTESS: Frau Bader is a good woman.

COUNT: Yes, she feels sorry for us. Ghastly.

COUNTESS: You still have a lot to learn.

COUNT: I finished my studies long ago.

COUNTESS: We're still at school, even if we're in a higher year now, perhaps we're already at university. (*Smiling.*) Take little Susanne for example, she's only just learning to read and write and like all children she's frightened of being left alone in the dark. We're not frightened any more, are we?

COUNT: You've become so brave.

(*He gives a slight smile.*)

COUNTESS: I've changed. Thank God.

COUNT: What does Susanne have to say?

COUNTESS: She wants to leave Figaro.

COUNT: (*Surprised.*) Leave him? Why?

COUNTESS: Because he's changed.

COUNT: Is he being unfaithful?

COUNTESS: No, but he only seems to be interested in the hairdressing salon and love's being neglected. (*She looks at the letter again.*) Poor Susanne! She's asking whether she could come back to us –

COUNT: To us?

COUNTESS: As lady's maid.

(*The COUNT grins.*)

She's yearning for the past.

(*Silence.*)

COUNT: (*Getting to his feet and pacing the room.*) By the way, the editor's written to say that there's no question of my memoirs being printed in the features section, not even in the Sunday supplement. An Almaviva offers his services and there's no question of them being accepted. His name is erased, his life dissolved. (*He takes the letter out of his pocket and reads it through again.*) What impertinence! My style is antiquated, these proles claim, when none of them knows how to construct a decent sentence these days – they're all a lot of hacks! There – take a look! (*He hands her his letter.*)

COUNTESS: (*Reads the letter and looks at the COUNT wide-eyed.*) Didn't you want to go to the café?

COUNT: I've no money.

COUNTESS: I've still got a bit – come on, off you go!

COUNT: And what d'you intend to eat this evening?

COUNTESS: There's something for you. I don't want to eat.

COUNT: You can't just go hungry.

COUNTESS: It's good for your health to fast once in a while – go on, go and play a bit of chess, take your mind off things –

COUNT: (*Smiling.*) It's like I'm your child. (*He puts his coat on and is about to leave but he stops by the door.*) And what are you going to say to Susanne?

COUNTESS: I'll write and tell her to keep her spirits up.

COUNT: And as far as our present financial circumstances are concerned you'll pass over all that –

COUNTESS: I will, I will.

(*She nods goodbye to him with a smile.*)

COUNT: Farewell. (*Exits.*)

COUNTESS: (*Taking a sheet of paper and writing.*) Dear Susanne, a woman's place is with her man –

Scene 3

In Grosshadersdorf. A week later. In the salon SUSANNE is attending FORESTER, a crafty son of the soil. She's lathering his face.

FORESTER: What are you doing this Thursday, Miss
  Susanne?

SUSANNE: What d'you mean, Mr Forester?

FORESTER: Thursday is New Year's Eve, the start of a new
  year.
  (*Silence.*)

SUSANNE: Me and my husband'll be going to the Post
  Hotel.

FORESTER: Then I'll go to the Post Hotel too. Do you
  like dancing?

SUSANNE: Yes, I do.

FORESTER: But we never see you at any parties or dances –

SUSANNE: No one knows how to dance in
  Grosshadersdorf.

FORESTER: That's true. I don't happen to come from
  Grosshadersdorf myself, I'm just stationed here.

SUSANNE: (*Smiling.*) Me too.

FORESTER: Then we're companions in misfortune. When
  I'm not out there in the woods, I get bored to death.

SUSANNE: (*Now shaving him.*) You're the only man who lets
  himself be shaved by me.

FORESTER: And your good husband?

SUSANNE: He shaves himself.
  (*Silence.*)

FORESTER: And where exactly is your husband?

SUSANNE: He's asleep. He always takes a nap after lunch.

FORESTER: And you don't take a nap?

SUSANNE: We take it in turns.

FORESTER: So you never sleep together?
  (*SUSANNE stops short, looks at him for a moment in horror,
  then goes on shaving him as if she hadn't heard.*)
  So, I'm the only person – the only one who lets you
  shave him?

SUSANNE: Yes, that's right.

FORESTER: Doesn't frighten me. I wouldn't mind having my throat slit by you.
(*He grins.*)

SUSANNE: (*With a forced laugh.*) Dear God, how gruesome! What would your good lady bride say to that? A bridegroom without a gullet.

FORESTER: She's got to get used to all sorts.
(*Silence.*)

SUSANNE: (*She's now finished shaving him.*) Hot or cold rub?

FORESTER: Hot and hotter than that. I like it really hot.
(*Suddenly he grabs her and brutally kisses her.*)

SUSANNE: (*Pulling away; under her breath.*) No! What d'you think you're doing?!

FORESTER: Only something that's completely natural. (*He gets up and moves slowly towards her.*)

SUSANNE: Leave me alone, you – you, or I really will slit your throat.

FORESTER: (*Interrupting her.*) Just slit away! (*He grabs her wrist in a flash and squeezes it.*)

SUSANNE: Ow! (*She drops the razor.*) You bastard, my husband's in there! If he wakes up! I'm going to scream – I'll scream –

FORESTER: (*Has now forced her into the corner.*) You just scream, no one's going to hear you, only me. (*Grabbing hold of her again and kissing her.*)

SUSANNE: (*Pulling away again and dropping a letter as she does so.*) You animal – bastard, now get out or I'll –
(*FORESTER does not move.
Silence.*)

FORESTER: (*Slowly turning away from her and putting on his fur coat.*) I'll catch up with you.

SUSANNE: Never.

FORESTER: Tomorrow. After the cinema.
(*SUSANNE doesn't answer.*)
I haven't paid yet.

SUSANNE: Forty.

FORESTER: (*Gives it to her.*) There you are.

SUSANNE: Thank you.

FORESTER: (*Pointing to the floor.*) There's a letter down
there. (*Exits.*)

SUSANNE: (*Slowly picking up the letter and mechanically
surveying its contents; then in a flat voice she reads.*) Dear
Susanne, a woman's place is with her man –
(*MIDWIFE enters carrying a small case.*)

MIDWIFE: And a very good day to you, Frau Figaro! Just
a quick bit of crimping then I must be on my way – (*She
sits down.*) And how is business?

SUSANNE: (*Attending to her.*) Thank you, we get by.

MIDWIFE: I hardly get a moment with all the work there
is. Five deliveries in one week. Two of them twins. Even
the toughest of men couldn't take that for long! If things
carry on like this our beloved Grosshadersdorf is going
to become a city of world renown and me with my poor
curls in a terrible state from all those storks flying about!
Positively an invasion! I've just come from the
headmaster's wife. The stork's just brought her a little
baby girl – a tiny bit premature, it's true, but she'll be a
source of joy to her mother, she's born under the right
signs, Capricorn and Mercury.

SUSANNE: You know about the stars, do you?

MIDWIFE: I know all about everything.

SUSANNE: What's May then?

MIDWIFE: In May Venus rules in the sign of the Bull. And
whose sign is that?

SUSANNE: Mine.

MIDWIFE: Oh yes? And what about your husband?

SUSANNE: Nobody knows. He's an orphan.

MIDWIFE: Ah! Well now! The stars don't play the same
role for our lords and masters; men change so quickly
but they're all shits; sometimes it's as if men don't have a
star sign at all. And how long have you been married,
young lady?

SUSANNE: Seven years.

MIDWIFE: Really? But it doesn't look like it.

SUSANNE: I got married at eighteen.

MIDWIFE: Just you be careful! The number seven has a
jinx on it. In every marriage there's a jinx every seven
years, that's just one of those magical metaphysical laws.
And why haven't you got any children? Running a top
business like this you really could afford to!

SUSANNE: And I'd like to, but it's my husband's fault.
(*Silence.*)

MIDWIFE: But you do live together as man and wife?

SUSANNE: Not very often. I've told him enough times that
I'll go to pieces if I don't have a child. But he doesn't
take any notice. Not a scrap.

MIDWIFE: There are ways of helping a husband along.
Believe you me I've had a hand in plenty of cases like
this. Now just listen. You go to your husband and you lie.
Tell him that his worst fears have borne fruit. And what
can he say to that? Nothing!

SUSANNE: You don't know my husband.

MIDWIFE: What can he do about it? *Force majeure!* He'll
feel Mother Nature has outwitted him and won't be
frightened any more once he realises there isn't any
point. That's the solution to your problem, in a nutshell:
anticipating the consequences. (*She gets up now
SUSANNE has finished crimping.*) And what do I owe you,
young lady?

SUSANNE: I'll be forever in your debt. Eighty, please.

MIDWIFE: (*Counting.*) We'll see one another again in
September. Mars and Libra, my congratulations!
Farewell, Frau Figaro!

SUSANNE: Goodbye, Madam.

FIGARO: (*Emerges from the private apartment wearing a
dressing gown and slippers; he is still half asleep; yawning he
takes off his dressing-gown then checks the till.*) One shave,
one set. (*To SUSANNE.*) Is that all?

SUSANNE: Yes.

FIGARO: It's funny more people don't want to get their
hair cut before the New Year, but they'll all come in in a
rush just before closing time on New Year's Eve so that
we lose half of them to the opposition – well that's life!

I'm going to give the matter another airing at the
Barbers' Association AGM. And it wouldn't do teachers
any harm if they explained to parents that you don't send
your kid to the barber's on a Saturday afternoon – I lose
some of my best beard-work just because some little
bastard turns up wanting a piddling haircut that earns
you peanuts. What's this razor doing on the floor? (*He
looks accusingly at SUSANNE.*) What sloppiness!

MIDWIFE: (*Coming back in a hurry.*) Didn't I leave my bag
here? Ah yes, there it is, thank goodness!

FIGARO: Everything is safe with us, Madam!

MIDWIFE: It would have been an expensive surprise, even
the stork would have raised an eyebrow. By the way,
talking of expensive surprises: have you heard the good
news Herr Figaro?

FIGARO: What good news?

SUSANNE: (*Suddenly.*) I haven't told him yet.

FIGARO: Don't know what you're on about.

SUSANNE: I just wasn't able to tell you.

FIGARO: What's that supposed to mean? There's nothing
in the world that you can't tell your husband, at any time
of the day or night. It's only after meals that I don't like
to be disturbed. (*To the MIDWIFE.*) Has she broken
something?

MIDWIFE: (*Smiling.*) On the contrary, Herr Figaro! It's a
happy event.

FIGARO: Happy event?

MIDWIFE: (*To SUSANNE.*) Courage! (*To FIGARO.*) A word
in your ear –
(*She whispers to him. FIGARO's eyes grow wider and he
keeps on glancing across at SUSANNE. She turns her back
on them both and, lost in thought, cleans the used razor.*)
There we are. (*To SUSANNE.*) Now it's out of the bag. (*To
FIGARO.*) My congratulations to you! Goodbye, young
lady! (*Exits.*)

FIGARO: (*Giving SUSANNE a stony glare; quietly.*) Is this
true?

SUSANNE: (*Without expression.*) Yes.

FIGARO: Who's the father?

SUSANNE: (*Spinning round.*) What d'you mean, who's the father? Do you really believe I could deceive you?

FIGARO: No, of course I don't believe that. Why on earth should you want to when you've got everything you want. Forgive me, I'm a bit confused. What a disaster!

SUSANNE: Disaster?

FIGARO: Am I supposed to rejoice perhaps?
(*Silence.*)

SUSANNE: You are a monster.

FIGARO: How often must I remind you that I am not a monster. I merely have a sense of responsibility and you know that I have the gift of prophecy. Am I supposed to look down from heaven above and watch my child die in the next war?

SUSANNE: I think you've got too great a sense of responsibility for Heaven. You'll go to Hell.

FIGARO: That's a matter I'd ask you to leave up to me! No one can have a child with a clear conscience in these times. Don't you read the newspapers? Each day someone else is killed – everyone's going to cop it eventually. Grosshadersdorf's about the safest place to live at the moment, relatively speaking, since there's no garrison here, no airport, nothing of strategic importance, in short nothing worth destroying. But they'll end up destroying what's worthless as well and the earthquakes'll see to the rest. We are living in an age of mass migrations, Susanne, and never have human beings been able to say with more justification than you and I: *après nous le deluge!* Bring your child into the world, go on, bring it! It'll live in a desolate lunar landscape with craters and poisonous rain – I must have a word with your friend the midwife, she'll know, what to do –

SUSANNE: (*Interrupting.*) Go ahead, go on, talk to her! I don't want your baby any more – And if I did have one I'd crawl away and hide like a bitch so that you wouldn't even know where your child had first seen the light of day, so that he wouldn't be cursed by you, since you don't even want him to live – I'd never let you see your

child, never! You don't deserve anything else, you're the
Kiss of Death, d'you hear, Death!

FIGARO: (*Looking round anxiously, he walks to the door, opens
it, then closes it again.*) Not so loud, Susanne! Let us at
least keep up appearances. People are already beginning
to talk –

SUSANNE: (*Interrupting him spitefully.*) Always 'people'
talking –

FIGARO: Yes, always, for ever and ever, amen.
(*Silence.*)

SUSANNE: (*Staring at him spitefully.*) You want to be left in
peace?

FIGARO: Right first time.

SUSANNE: (*Slowly and maliciously.*) Then I'll simplify the
argument. Figaro, I lied to you just now. I'm not
expecting your baby –

FIGARO: (*With a start.*) What?! There isn't a baby?!

SUSANNE: I only said I was so you'd at last take pity on
me. It was just a trick –

FIGARO: A trick?

SUSANNE: Your wife wanted to trick you so that she might
become a mother through you, you, her lord and master.
But it's all over now. The man she wanted to have a child
by doesn't live in Grosshadersdorf.

FIGARO: Do me a favour!

SUSANNE: I dreamt about him last night. He leaned over
me and his shadow was three times the size of the earth.
I could see him so clearly.

FIGARO: Who?

SUSANNE: My one true love.
(*Silence.*)

FIGARO: What's his name?

SUSANNE: He's dead.
(*Silence.*)

FIGARO: Who was he?

SUSANNE: He was called Figaro.

FIGARO: Figaro?!

SUSANNE: Yes, my Figaro looked forward to the future
when there was a thunderstorm and he leapt to the

window when the lightning struck, but you? You won't even leave the house without an umbrella! My Figaro went to prison because he wrote what he believed, you wouldn't even dare to read in secret the things that he wrote! My Figaro would be the first to confront Count Almaviva with the truth, at the height of his powers, you just keep up appearances in Grosshadersdorf! You are a narrow-minded petty bourgeois, he was a citizen of the world. He was a man and you –

FIGARO: Whether or not I am a man is hardly something you just realise one day after seven years of marriage. I however do now realise that you are a swindler and not a mother, more chambermaid than business-woman, always in front of a mirror and yet sloppy in your work, vain, flirtatious, whining, superficial –

SUSANNE: (*Interrupting him.*) Superficial? Did you say superficial?

FIGARO: (*Grinning.*) Superficial or not, we know one another inside and out.

SUSANNE: Once you used to know but now you've forgotten everything.

HEADMASTER: (*Enters.*) Haircut please! Good day, my pretty lady!

(*SUSANNE runs off sobbing into their apartment. The HEADMASTER watches her, perplexed.*)

What's the matter with her?

FIGARO: Just a mood.

Scene 4

Big New Year's Eve celebration at the Post Hotel. SUSANNE has withdrawn into an empty side-room. In the neighbouring hall dance, music is playing. On the wall a clock and a poster for the New Year's Eve Tombola. The FORESTER comes out of the hall. He is wearing evening dress.

FORESTER: I've been looking for you everywhere! What are you doing sitting out here? It'll be the New Year in twenty minutes.

SUSANNE: (*In a flat voice.*) Shall we dance?

FORESTER: No.

(*SUSANNE stares at him wide-eyed.*)

I just wanted to tell you that I can't dance with you any more. People were watching us last night after the cinema. I've only just found out. They know you were with me at my place. We must deny everything.

SUSANNE: (*In a flat voice.*) So?

FORESTER: Aren't you upset?!

SUSANNE: I'd guessed as much.

FORESTER: Guessed?

SUSANNE: I'd expected that we wouldn't be able to dance any more – (*She gets up.*) He didn't deserve any better.

FORESTER: (*Pricking up his ears.*) Who?

SUSANNE: Figaro. Yes, I must go.

FORESTER: (*Suspiciously.*) Where to?

SUSANNE: Away from Figaro.

(*Pause.*)

FORESTER: That's very nice! Need grounds for divorce?

(*SUSANNE stares at him in consternation.*)

So it was only because you wanted to get away from him that you came to the cinema with me? Forcing me into a frivolous adultery as a means to your own ends, were you?

SUSANNE: (*Shouting at him.*) That's not true!

FORESTER: Don't you shout at me! If you compromise me any further this evening then I'll really drop you in it and you wouldn't be the first one –

SUSANNE: (*Interrupting him but in a measured voice.*) Go on, kill me.

FORESTER: So you want to make me a murderer as well, do you?

SUSANNE: Perhaps you'd enjoy that – (*She smiles.*)

FORESTER: (*Shaking her.*) Pull yourself together!

(*Silence.*)

SUSANNE: (*Uncannily calm and precise.*) I came back to your place because I fancied you.

(*FORESTER stares at her. SUSANNE as before.*)

That is all.

FORESTER: That's all? You destroy my prospects of marriage: what decent citizens would knowingly entrust their daughter to the local adulterer? And that's nothing to you?! But I'll deny everything! Everything!

(*He hurries off into the hall. SUSANNE, alone; she stares gloomily into space, then takes out a small mirror from her handbag and powders her face. FIGARO comes out of the hall. He is wearing a shabby tail-coat. SUSANNE takes no notice of him.*)

FIGARO: Come along, Susanne.

SUSANNE: No.

FIGARO: And why not, may one ask?

SUSANNE: It's too smoky in there.

FIGARO: In twenty minutes it'll be the New Year.

SUSANNE: I'll choke before then.

(*Pause.*)

FIGARO: Susanne, we must pay heed to what people think. Let us at least keep up appearances.

SUSANNE: I don't give a shit about your appearances.

(*HEADMASTER comes out of the hall with ADALBERT, the pastry-cook, and BASIL, the butcher.*)

FIGARO: (*To SUSANNE.*) People are coming! Control yourself! (*To the two men.*) In what way may I be of assistance, gentlemen?

BASIL: Hello, Figaro! You certainly made a pig's ear of my hair today!

FIGARO: Impossible!

ADALBERT: That's what comes of being distracted.

(*He gives SUSANNE a withering look.*)

FIGARO: I shall of course repair the cut, Herr Basil.

BASIL: You can repair everything, even the worst crack in a marriage, but not hair-cuts! The hair's got to be given a chance to grow again first!

(*He laughs menacingly and ADALBERT laughs too, but the HEADMASTER remains serious.*)

FIGARO: (*Makes a bow to ADALBERT in some confusion and turns to SUSANNE; under his breath.*) Now move! (*Out loud.*) May I have the pleasure? (*Under his breath.*) Now I've even botched a hair-cut –

(*He accompanies SUSANNE into the hall.*)

ADALBERT: Well now. Alone at last – (*He takes out a bottle of brandy and three glasses that he had hidden in his coat and places them on the table; he fills the glasses.*) My good lady wife fears that I'll have a heart attack if I have a drink – I reckon that if she were to come in now she'd be the one to have the heart attack, that's what I reckon – (*He grins.*)

BASIL: (*Grinning.*) Don't tempt fate, my dear old friend! What are we drinking to, then, gentlemen?

HEADMASTER: To your little daughter, Herr Basil!

ADALBERT: Bravo!

(*The gentlemen drink their toast.*)

BASIL: D'you think the barber's twigged yet?

ADALBERT: Hardly likely. He's still talking to her.

BASIL: Well, if my wife had cheated on me I'd stick a knife in her just like that – but with some jumped-up little hairdresser you never know what he'll get up to. Lets his wife cheat on him left, right and centre and then he takes her to the ball!

HEADMASTER: He's keeping up appearances.

BASIL: Ha, what d'you mean appearances! People like that don't have no sense of honour in them – bloody disgrace it is!

HEADMASTER: And if he were to stick a knife in his Susanne now I wouldn't like to know what you'd be saying then! Nothing's ever right for us in Grosshadersdorf. But we've got our weak spots too.

BASIL: And we can afford to have them, Mr Teacher, and our weak spots are no concern of anybody's, but some jumped-up little shit like him had better watch his step if he wants to get on here in our town!

ADALBERT: I always say it's women, the real masters, who're to blame for everything. They're the ones who bring you into the world and the ones who see you into the grave.

(*JOSEPHA comes out of the dance-hall with the MIDWIFE.*)

Christ, it's my wife!

(*He behaves as if he hadn't seen her and whispers to BASIL and the HEADMASTER.*)

JOSEPHA: (*To the MIDWIFE.*) Ah, so there he is, God's gift to women. I never let him out of my sight. If I do he'll drink himself silly and then have a heart attack and I'll have all the mess to clear up – looks like a good start to the New Year!
(*The gentlemen laugh out loud and then start to whisper again.*)

MIDWIFE: The gentlemen are telling one another jokes.

JOSEPHA: Now it's my husband's turn. I know the joke, it's the only one he knows and he tells it year in year out. No one'll laugh.
(*The gentlemen roar with laughter.*)

MIDWIFE: Perhaps you don't know all the jokes your better half tells?

JOSEPHA: (*Gives the MIDWIFE a withering look and then calls out.*) Adalbert! Adalbert!

ADALBERT: (*Sighs and comes over to her.*) What's the matter now, Josepha?

JOSEPHA: (*Reproachfully.*) You told a joke and they all laughed –

ADALBERT: That wasn't a joke! We were only talking about the hairdresser's wife!

BASIL: (*Shouting to JOSEPHA.*) Yesterday she cheated on her Figaro! (*He laughs.*)

MIDWIFE: (*Horrified.*) She did what?

ADALBERT: Absolutely. No doubt about it.

BASIL: After the cinema.

MIDWIFE: I don't believe it!

JOSEPHA: And why shouldn't you believe it? Doesn't surprise me one bit! She's capable of anything, that stuck-up bitch; she's got adulteress written all over her! (*To BASIL.*) And who was the lucky man?

ADALBERT: The forester.

JOSEPHA: (*Taken aback.*) With a fine upright man like that? It's scandalous! She seduced him, that Jezebel!

HEADMASTER: (*Getting up in obvious embarrassment.*) I wouldn't exactly say that he took a great deal of seducing –

JOSEPHA: You just don't understand women, Headmaster! I know this young forester well and I also know how bashful he is in his dealings with women; he's a fine, modest man and he comes from a good family! I've been saying for ages that these foreigners should never have been allowed in, they're corrupting our whole moral climate!

BASIL: That's right!

JOSEPHA: He's just about tolerable but her – she's poison!

BASIL: He's worthless too! Look what a pig's ear he made of my hair!

FIGARO: (*Enters from the dance-hall; he is clearly beside himself but controlled; to ADALBERT.*) Sir, I've been looking for you, sir. You claimed that my wife cheated on me yesterday –

ADALBERT: (*Cowardly.*) Me? I didn't claim anything!

MIDWIFE: Of course he did –

JOSEPHA: (*Furiously interrupting what the MIDWIFE is saying.*) I'll thank you not to go meddling in affairs that don't concern you, thank you very much! (*To FIGARO.*) My husband never claimed any such thing, d'you hear? Neither yesterday, nor today, nor tomorrow. And when you go sounding off like that you get my husband so worked up that he will have that heart attack, but you can kiss goodbye to us as customers!

FIGARO: I don't give a damn! My wife's honour has been impugned and I demand an explanation!

BASIL: (*Interrupting him noisily.*) You don't have any right to make demands here! You're nothing but a dirty foreigner. Demands, demands – that really is too much! You should be glad we were so hospitable to you here and that we let you butcher our hair, you jumped-up refugee you... If we didn't subsidise you then you'd have snuffed it by now!

JOSEPHA: That's right! And he's insolent with it!

BASIL: (*To the HEADMASTER.*) Let's go, Schoolteacher!

HEADMASTER: (*Suddenly yelling at BASIL.*) I am not a schoolteacher, my title as far as you are concerned is Headmaster, d'you hear?

(*He exits quickly into the hall.*)

JOSEPHA: (*To ADALBERT.*) Come along, Adalbert!

(*She exits with him into the hall.*)

BASIL: Bloody schoolteacher, I'll fix him – (*To the MIDWIFE.*) And as for you, the only reason you take sides with jumped-up jerks like that is because you're the only midwife we've got, so you've no competition! Serve you right if we all died!

(*He exits into the hall. FIGARO gazes stonily into space.*)

MIDWIFE: Herr Figaro, don't take any notice of those people, they're a bad lot, I know them all. Trust your wife, but you must change your attitude towards her.

FIGARO: (*Tonelessly.*) And what is my attitude?

MIDWIFE: The wrong one. She loves you very much, you know –

FORESTER: (*Coming out of the hall.*) Herr Figaro!

(*FIGARO turns round with a start.*)

I heard there was a row going on in here. I'd like to tell you something, man to man: I've had a good number of women in my life but never once a married woman. Out of a certain sense of male solidarity I'd never do something like that. Being a friend of the family's not in my line, I just happened to meet your wife at the cinema – that's all.

FIGARO: Word of honour?

FORESTER: Cross my heart.

MIDWIFE: Well, there we are!

(*It is beginning to grow dark, the New Year is about to begin, greeted with yells and shrieks. Twelve chimes. Shouts of 'Cheers'. When the lights come on again the music being played is a rousing march; in the sideroom FIGARO and SUSANNE stand facing one another. They are alone.*)

SUSANNE: Happy New Year, Figaro.

FIGARO: Happy New Year. Susanne, it was nasty of me to be suspicious like that. Forgive me.

SUSANNE: I've nothing to forgive you for. Figaro, I've been unfaithful to you.

End of Act Two.

ACT THREE

Scene 1

Six months later. In the offices of the International League for the Assistance of Refugees. Its General Secretary, a DOCTOR of law, is forty years old and a chain-smoker. Her face is as grey as the heaps of unprocessed files lying on the upper shelves of the office and reaching up as far as the ceiling. She is in the process of dictating an appeal to her SECRETARY who is taking it down in shorthand.

FRÄULEIN DOCTOR: Now where was I?

SECRETARY: You'd just got to humanity.

FRÄULEIN DOCTOR: Ah yes. Right: 'In the name of humanity the International League for the Assistance of Refugees appeals, across all boundaries of party, race, creed and class, to the goodness of your hearts. Help to soften the cruel fate of the *émigrés*, for it is a fate to which they have been exposed without protection. Emigration destroys everything: Faith, Hope, Charity – how many of them fall into despair, lose heart, or commit suicide! We appeal to every one of you, you who have the good fortune still to possess a homeland and who cannot imagine what a tragedy it would be to lose it, to help us with a donation. Join the International League for the Assistance of Refugees. Help, help, help! Account Number et cetera.' That's it. Full stop. Have we any aspirin left?

SECRETARY: No we haven't, Fräulein Doctor.

FRÄULEIN DOCTOR: My head's pounding again. I've got a headache you could photograph.

SECRETARY: Perhaps you shouldn't smoke so much.

FRÄULEIN DOCTOR: I don't feel human if I don't smoke. Is there anyone out there?

SECRETARY: A man and a woman.

FRÄULEIN DOCTOR: Clients?

SECRETARY: I've already told them we don't have any
money. But they're not asking for money –

FRÄULEIN DOCTOR: (*Interrupting her.*) Well, send them
in!

(*SECRETARY exits. FRÄULEIN DOCTOR nervously lights
another cigarette.*)

COUNT: (*Enters with SUSANNE and makes a short bow.*)
Permit me to introduce myself. Count Almaviva –

FRÄULEIN DOCTOR: (*Offering them a seat.*) Please do sit
down!

(*They sit down.*)

How can I be of assistance?

COUNT: It concerns this girl, that's to say this young lady,
whom I've known for more than ten years now, and I'd
put my hand in the fire for her –

FRÄULEIN DOCTOR: (*Interrupting him.*) Forgive me, who
did you say you were?

COUNT: Count Almaviva.

FRÄULEIN DOCTOR: (*With a smile.*) Sorry, the name
doesn't mean anything –

COUNT: (*With a smile.*) Please don't worry. I've long since
grown accustomed to not meaning anything – to be
brief: once upon a time I was a wealthy man and this
young lady was my wife's maid. She emigrated with us,
but later we split up; then however she wanted to come
back to us but we were already living elsewhere – (*He
smiles; to SUSANNE.*) You had to look for us for quite a
while, eh?

(*SUSANNE nods in agreement.*)

(*To the FRÄULEIN DOCTOR.*) Yes, and now of course we
can't afford a lady's maid, but I did manage, thanks to
my former connections, to find a nice little position for
my protégée. She's a waitress now, her boss is an *émigré*
too, his name's Herr von Cherubin. He used to be my
page-boy back in the Stone Age.

FRÄULEIN DOCTOR: (*Growing impatient.*) Well, if your
protégée's got a job then everything's fine and dandy!

COUNT: Wrong! Very wrong, because the young lady is
stateless and needs a work-permit –

FRÄULEIN DOCTOR: I see. The same old story. (*To SUSANNE.*) Are you married?

SUSANNE: I'm divorced, got the decree absolute.

FRÄULEIN DOCTOR: And where does your former husband live?

SUSANNE: Not a clue. Haven't the faintest.

COUNT: He left her.

FRÄULEIN DOCTOR: What is your husband, anyway?

SUSANNE: What he is now I've no idea. At one time or another he was everything.

COUNT: At one time he was also my valet.

SUSANNE: When we split up he was a hairdresser in Grosshadersdorf, but shortly after our separation the salon went into liquidation. The locals didn't want any more to do with him.

FRÄULEIN DOCTOR: And why not?

SUSANNE: They won't tolerate a divorced man if he's a foreigner.

FRÄULEIN DOCTOR: Does he support you?

SUSANNE: No.

FRÄULEIN DOCTOR: He left you and is the guilty party?

SUSANNE: No, I'm the guilty party.
(*Silence.*)

FRÄULEIN DOCTOR: Do you have children?

SUSANNE: (*Shaking her head.*) Thank God!

FRÄULEIN DOCTOR: That I can understand.
(*Silence.*)

COUNT: (*To the FRÄULEIN DOCTOR.*) And as far as the work permit's concerned?

FRÄULEIN DOCTOR: (*Interrupting him.*) I very much hope we can do something, really. A temporary one, perhaps.

COUNT: Bravo!

FRÄULEIN DOCTOR: (*Defensively.*) A work permit is often granted only to be subsequently rescinded – (*She hands SUSANNE a sheet of paper.*) Fill out this form and make sure you do it properly!

(*SUSANNE sits down at a small table and begins filling out the form.*)

COUNT: (*To the FRAULEIN DOCTOR.*) Excuse me, there is another private matter – does the League for Assistance have a legal department?

FRÄULEIN DOCTOR: Do you need information on a point of law?

COUNT: Yes.

FRÄULEIN DOCTOR: I'm a doctor of law. How can I help?

COUNT: (*With an embarrassed look at SUSANNE.*) Can we please talk quietly?

FRÄULEIN DOCTOR: As you wish.

COUNT: Recently I've been spending some time acting for clients, you know, property, buying and selling, but unfortunately I had a bit of bad luck – (*He stops and hands over some letters and documents to her.*) Please would you be so kind as to cast your eye over –

FRÄULEIN DOCTOR: (*Studies the papers, stops short and looks at the COUNT in amazement; then very quietly.*) You mean to say that you wrote these?

COUNT: Yes.

(*Silence.*)

FRÄULEIN DOCTOR: And this too?

COUNT: But of course.

(*Silence.*)

FRÄULEIN DOCTOR: So you sold something that didn't belong to you?

COUNT: Excuse me, but I sold it only on the strict understanding that I was merely acting on behalf of a client and as such was compelled to act as I did –

FRÄULEIN DOCTOR: (*Cutting in.*) Compelled or not compelled, it's still fraud.

COUNT: D'you really think so?

FRÄULEIN DOCTOR: Misappropriation and outright deceit.

COUNT: Is it really? But my client assured me expressly that it was nothing illegal –

FRÄULEIN DOCTOR: Come come now, Count. A child could've seen that.

COUNT: But he gave me his word of honour.

FRÄULEIN DOCTOR: And you believed him?

SUSANNE: (*Suddenly addressing the FRÄULEIN DOCTOR.*) Excuse me, but do I cross out the bits that are not applicable or underline the ones that are?

FRÄULEIN DOCTOR: As you like –

SUSANNE: I'll cross out the bits that aren't.
(*She crosses them out. Silence.*)

FRÄULEIN DOCTOR: (*To the COUNT.*) Have you been in trouble before?

COUNT: No.
(*Silence.*)

FRÄULEIN DOCTOR: I'd advise you to make a clean breast of it.

COUNT: (*With a strange smile.*) And what would one gain from that?

FRÄULEIN DOCTOR: Hmm, well now. I'd say, anything up to three years.

COUNT: Three years!

FRÄULEIN DOCTOR: (*Holding a letter in each hand and weighing them up.*) Need versus negligence. The aggravating circumstances outweigh the mitigating ones.
(*Silence.*)

COUNT: My wife always says we're still at school waiting for the summer holidays to begin – (*He gazes heavenwards.*) Is there long to wait, Sir?

Scene 2

Six months later in the land of the Revolution, at the former palace of the exiled COUNT ALMAVIVA. In front of the beautiful baroque entrance gate ANTONIO, formerly the castle gardener, and PEDRILLO, one-time groom to the COUNT and now castle warden, are sitting in the sunshine. The former is smoking, the latter reading the newspaper. It's the middle of summer.

ANTONIO: Anything in the paper?

PEDRILLO: Things are progressing.

ANTONIO: Where?

PEDRILLO: Here. Everywhere else in the world there's a rapidly deepening recession, only here are we experiencing strong economic growth.

ANTONIO It'd be all right if you could see it –

PEDRILLO: You are a dangerous dissident. Upon my soul, if you weren't my very own father-in-law I'd have hauled you up before the Revolutionary Tribunal long ago.

ANTONIO: Haul me up, my dear son-in-law. I'm an old man and I shan't live long and what I'd say to your good friends in the Tribunal is: the days when his Honour Count Almaviva was still living here, those days are gone, they'll never come again.

PEDRILLO: Thank goodness!

ANTONIO Those were better days.

PEDRILLO: Really? And what about the countless crimes committed by your noble Count Almaviva? Have you forgotten what shameful and outrageous acts this noble villain has to his credit, eh? I'll just remind you of the brutality and selfishness with which he cynically indulged his seigneurial rights. The poor young girls on the estate were just fair game for his baser instincts, even that Susanne, the wife of his personal valet, nearly had to succumb, and if she had, it'd have served him right, that bastard Figaro, that traitor to the cause of the people! Helping the Count over the border, a count whose sole aim is to gratify his animal instincts! Sarcastical old bugger!

ANTONIO: If we'd been counts I reckon we'd have gratified ours too –

PEDRILLO: But we were not counts, thank you very much. You were his exploited, tormented castle gardener.

ANTONIO: (*Interrupting him.*) What was I? Is that what I was? Tormented?

PEDRILLO: You had to grow the most exotic vegetables for the Countess's fancy dinners – and your dinners? You had to eat nothing but cabbage, day in, day out!

ANTONIO: (*Grinning nastily.*) Cabbage keeps you frisky.

PEDRILLO: (*Yelling at him.*) But I detest cabbage, d'you hear? Cabbage and carrots, I can't stand either of them! (*Some children run past, laughing and shouting; they are playing with a ball and the ball hits ANTONIO.*)

ANTONIO: (*Looks at the children angrily.*) Cheeky bastards –

PEDRILLO: They're not bastards, they're pupils at the State Orphanage in the former castle of His Grace the Count and you just get that into your thick skull! Where once effete generations played frivolous games, now a strong new race is being bred for the future, lively, liberated and hard as steel.

ANTONIO: Your steely new race being bred for the future recently stole all my apples –

PEDRILLO: You're nothing but a nasty old nihilist!

ANTONIO: (*Erupting.*) I won't stand for your insults! Who d'you think you are? The most stupid castle warden that ever lived! All you can see is the 'future', the 'future'! The fact that there's all those art treasures rotting in the cellar, all those paintings, furniture, tapestries, you couldn't give a shit! It breaks my heart when I think of what's in those cellars!

PEDRILLO: A live human being is worth more to me than all the dead art in the world.

ANTONIO: Did you pick that up from some book you've read?

PEDRILLO: If I were as illiterated as you are I'd feel sorry for myself!

FANCHETTE: (*Runs in bursting with excitement.*) Pedrillo, Pedrillo!

PEDRILLO: Where's the fire?

FANCHETTE: Guess what I just saw – I was standing in the park, by the fountain of Neptune –

PEDRILLO: (*Interrupting her.*) There is no fountain of Neptune, only a September the twenty-third fountain, and just you remember that!

FANCHETTE: It's not important.

PEDRILLO: Oh, isn't it? That's my wife talking – (*To ANTONIO.*) Your daughter!

ANTONIO: Get stuffed.

PEDRILLO: Stuff yourself. (*To FANCHETTE.*) Go on.

FANCHETTE: Don't you order me about, I'm not one of your guards! Anyway there I am standing by the twenty-third Neptune fountain when somebody comes towards me over the meadow. For a moment my heart stopped beating, I thought I'd seen a ghost!

ANTONIO: A ghost?

FANCHETTE: (*To ANTONIO.*) In broad daylight!

PEDRILLO: (*To FANCHETTE.*) There are no such things as supernatural beings. Go on!

FANCHETTE: It wasn't a supernatural being, it was a completely sensuous human being made of flesh and blood – an old acquaintance!

PEDRILLO: Who was it?

FANCHETTE: You're not going to believe me –

PEDRILLO: Well, go on, tell us then!

FANCHETTE: It was Figaro.

ANTONIO: Figaro?!

PEDRILLO: What? That miserable refugee daring to show his face here? That's what I call showing contempt, impudence personified, the provocation of the century, outrageous.

FANCHETTE: Please don't be so pretentious!

PEDRILLO: (*Gazing at her.*) Perhaps it wouldn't suit you if I had him locked up?

FANCHETTE: Are you jealous again?

PEDRILLO: Jealous of a refugee? You must be joking!

FIGARO: (*Comes in and stops.*) Ah! There you are –
(*He smiles. All three of them remain expressionless.*)
Hello, Fanchette!

PEDRILLO: (*Darkly.*) Good day to you.

FIGARO: (*To PEDRILLO.*) Nice to see you. How are you?

ANTONIO: Not good.
(*Silence.*)

PEDRILLO: (*Grimly.*) We weren't expecting you.

FIGARO: So you're surprised, are you?

PEDRILLO: (*With a grim smile.*) Very pleasantly so too –
(*Shouting at FIGARO.*) Bloody refugees, that's all we
needed!
(*Silence.*)

FIGARO: (*Suddenly.*) Bye! (*He starts to go.*)

PEDRILLO: Stay where you are! You know what's coming!

FIGARO: (*Smiling.*) There can't be much coming for me –

PEDRILLO: Oh no?

FIGARO: When it comes down to it I only left because of
my wife. I emigrated for love – (*He grins.*)

PEDRILLO: Love is a private matter to do with the
anarchy of the individual; politically we couldn't give a
shit about your individual behaviour.

FANCHETTE: And where's Susanne?

FIGARO: No idea.

FANCHETTE: (*Puzzled.*) How come?

FIGARO: We're divorced.

FANCHETTE: Divorced?!

FIGARO: Decree absolute. Six months ago.

FANCHETTE: Were you unfaithful to her?

FIGARO: On the contrary! And vice versa.

FANCHETTE: (*Unable to take it in.*) She was unfaithful to
you?

FIGARO: That's right.

PEDRILLO: (*Casting a glance at FANCHETTE; grins grimly
at FIGARO.*) Well I never!

FANCHETTE: (*To herself.*) Poor Susanne!

PEDRILLO: Who was the lucky man? (*Casting another
glance at FANCHETTE.*) The Count?

FIGARO: (*Smiling.*) Oh no, only a forester, a mere mortal –

PEDRILLO: There are neither mere mortals nor any other
kind of mortals, there are just mortals and that's that,
understand, you alien?

FIGARO: Who are you calling an 'alien'? I'm no alien,
d'you hear! I'm an orphan it's true and I don't know
whether I was born here or not but I was certainly found
here, that I do know –

PEDRILLO: Worst luck.

FIGARO: Whether you like it or not I'm as at home here as the trees, the fields, the water and the air, understand?

PEDRILLO: (*Threateningly.*) Don't you go shouting at me. A refugee's always an alien and he doesn't have such a thing as a home because he's betrayed it.

FIGARO: I've betrayed bugger all, you great idiot! I remember a certain Pedrillo who was the Count's groom and without the services of a certain Figaro you'd still be stable-boy! Just who was it gave you the first book in which it was written black on white that a servant doesn't always have to remain a servant?! Who did you learn about the Revolution from? From me, from a certain Figaro!

PEDRILLO: (*Yelling at him.*) But without the services of a certain Figaro the Count would never have escaped me – who was it got him over the border, eh? You, you traitor! If my sense of revolutionary discipline weren't so strong, I'd thump you one right now!

FANCHETTE: Oh, do stop arguing like that!

PEDRILLO: (*To FANCHETTE.*) Don't you go poking your nose in or there'll be even more trouble!

FIGARO: What's the Count ever done to you?

PEDRILLO: He raped my wife.

FIGARO: (*In confusion.*) Raped? (*With a questioning glance in FANCHETTE's direction.*)
(*FANCHETTE smiles in embarrassment and behind PEDRILLO's back she indicates that it wasn't that bad.*)

PEDRILLO: If I'd caught a certain Count in the act I'd have given him something to think about. (*He strikes the air.*) Like that and that and that! (*With a withering glance at FIGARO.*) Now I'm going to fetch the guards. (*Exits.*)

FANCHETTE: (*To FIGARO.*) Please run for it, please! My husband's got no mercy once he gets the bit between his teeth. You wouldn't believe how he can hate!

ANTONIO: He's a raging beast –

FANCHETTE: (*Shouting at ANTONIO.*) Don't talk about him as though he were an animal all the time, Papa. Even Pedrillo has his good points, he believes in our cause! (*To FIGARO.*) Figaro, for the sake of our former friendship I beg of you to go! He'll have you put in jail and you'll lose your head!!

FIGARO: My head? The days when the head played no part in things, those days are gone. Today the good old head is trumps again and death sentences are passed only to be rescinded. The 'executed' throng onto the floor of the Stock Exchange and give the executioner bad tips – (*He smiles.*) No, Fanchette, Figaro's staying. He left Grosshadersdorf and took the road to Damascus. But in Damascus there are just more Grosshadersdorfers, except they have a different postcode –

PEDRILLO: (*Returning with the guards; to FIGARO.*) Figaro, in the name of the people I now declare you under arrest.

FIGARO: Just a moment! (*To the SERGEANT.*) Before you go to the trouble of putting me in chains, let me give you a piece of good advice. Have a look at this – (*He hands the SERGEANT a document.*) I'd like to spare you, sir, the disgrace I would be happy to see that gentleman in – (*Pointing to PEDRILLO.*)

PEDRILLO: (*Confused.*) What's that supposed to mean then?

(*As the SERGEANT reads the document his eyes open wider and wider.*)

FIGARO: (*To PEDRILLO.*) I wouldn't have wanted to see you in disgrace, if you hadn't been so mercilessly stupid. (*To the SERGEANT.*) Sergeant, have you managed to decipher the document?

SERGEANT: Yes sir! (*He gives orders to the guard.*) Stand to a-ttention! Pre-sent arms! Eyes left!

(*The guard presents arms to FIGARO.*)

PEDRILLO: What's that? You're presenting arms to him?!

SERGEANT: (*To PEDRILLO.*) Silence!

PEDRILLO: 'Silence'? Am I going mad?

FIGARO: (*To PEDRILLO.*) Just a moment! It's all up, Pedrillo. There it is, black on white – (*He hands the document over to him.*) You are retired.

PEDRILLO: (*Almost having a heart attack.*) Retired?

FANCHETTE: Who?!

PEDRILLO: Me?!

FIGARO: Yes, you.

ANTONIO: (*To himself.*) About time too!

FANCHETTE: (*To PEDRILLO.*) Give it to me –
(*She rips the document out of his hand and hastily reads it with him.*)

FIGARO: (*To the SERGEANT.*) Thank you, Sergeant!

SERGEANT: (*Giving the order to the guard.*) Eyes front! Left turn! March! (*He exits with the guard.*)

PEDRILLO: (*Having now read the document he screams out.*) What's this?! Is this really happening – you, you're the new castle warden?

FIGARO: (*To FANCHETTE who is staring at him open-mouthed.*) That's right. Why should I make an honest living there shaving and trimming when I can become castle warden back here if I use a bit of nous. No, I left here, stealthily under cover of darkness as if I'd been an aristocrat and not a servant at all – yes, it was love that lulled me into it, I was asleep, dreaming of the blue yonder – but now I'm wide awake again, I'm all here, and have been for the last three weeks. I have put my services at the disposal of the new lords and masters, confessed all to them, and they have forgiven me my 'sins of emigration', even though I wasn't especially overcome with remorse – (*He grins.*) Yes, yes indeed, the Revolution has acquired a more human face, a favourable base for those of an independent nature who're looking for the second joker in the pack –

PEDRILLO: Those of an independent nature are carving out niches for themselves!

FIGARO: Don't you talk to me about independent natures!

PEDRILLO: What crime have I committed to be hacked down so swiftly? Am I too revolutionary perhaps?!

FIGARO: (*Very softly so that the guard can't overhear.*) Quite apart from that you made a bad miscalculation.

PEDRILLO: What d'you mean, miscalculation?

FIGARO: You've been looking after forty-eight orphans here in the Children's Home, but you've always managed to get the figure back to front and call it eighty-four. And, noble knight, you can thank me for the fact that I'm not having you arrested.

FANCHETTE: (*To PEDRILLO.*) You see, I always told you it'd come out some day.

PEDRILLO: You shut your mouth! Who bought that piano on the never-never? You or me?

FANCHETTE: And who was it drank the never-never down the pub? You or me?

FIGARO: Don't get worked up about it all, my good people. You only did what all castle wardens do. I've got a thing or two I'd like to say.

ANTONIO: (*Aside.*) I've got a thing or two I'd like to say as well, but you won't catch me saying 'em!

FANCHETTE: And what about Susanne?

FIGARO: Susanne? Doesn't exist any longer, that's how she wanted it, she was unfaithful to me.

FANCHETTE: And she was right too.

FIGARO: Really?

FANCHETTE: If it doesn't matter to you whether or not she's out there begging, then she was certainly right to be unfaithful. There are two kinds of right, you see, like this or like that.
(*FIGARO stops short and looks at her wide-eyed.*
FANCHETTE continues slowly and as if waiting.)
And why was your Susanne unfaithful to you then?

FIGARO: What d'you mean, why? We'd grown apart from one another –

FANCHETTE: Just like that, 'apart' – and whose fault was that?

FIGARO: Not mine.

FANCHETTE: So you were completely innocent, were you?
(*PEDRILLO gives a nasty laugh.*)

FIGARO: I was always faithful to her.

FANCHETTE: That doesn't prove anything.

FIGARO: (*Sharply.*) Doesn't it?

FANCHETTE: You still don't have any children, I suppose?

FIGARO: No, thank God.

FANCHETTE: Poor Susanne! There's no sense in being a woman if you don't have children.

FIGARO: There's no sense in a lot of things these days.

FANCHETTE: But becoming castle warden that's still worth doing, eh, Mr Innocence?

(*Silence.*)

You should be ashamed of yourself. You're more corrupt than we are. Yes, you're corrupt, through and through.

FIGARO: Am I really?

ANTONIO: (*To FANCHETTE.*) Let him have his fun!

FIGARO: (*To ANTONIO.*) Just let her alone! (*To FANCHETTE.*) Go on.

FANCHETTE: I'd go on whether you let me or not, Mr Castle Warden.

(*Silence.*)

FIGARO: (*To FANCHETTE.*) Just you listen to me! Since Susanne was unfaithful I've learned a good deal; no man is more hated nor more despised in this world than an honest man with a brain. There's only one way out. You have to make a decision; honesty or intelligence. If you choose honesty, you have to make sacrifices, if you choose intelligence then others make the sacrifices. I've made my decision.

ANTONIO: Bravo!

PEDRILLO: Just you listen to me, Figaro, before I go off to the pub: I'd just like to say to you in all seriousness that I fought for a great cause, even if I did fiddle the books, but that doesn't affect the cause and that cause will always progress inexorably forwards, even if every castle warden were to fiddle the books!

ANTONIO: (*With a throwaway gesture.*) 'Progress inexorably'!

FIGARO: (*Shouting at ANTONIO.*) Don't you go imagining that our good Count Almaviva wasn't corrupt, he was undoubtedly just as enthusiastic about his book-fiddling as we are, it's just that with him you didn't notice it any more because people had got used to it generations ago – his kind of corruption had as it were become an established right!

PEDRILLO: It's true!

FIGARO: Who was our good Count anyway? A man of substance who imagined he had a brain of substance! 'In two months it'll all be over!' Drivel! Birth, wealth, class and rank made him proud! And what had he done, our good Count, to earn so many advantages? He took the bother to be born and that was the only work he ever did in his life, the rest of it he frittered, fopped and fiddled away.

PEDRILLO: How very true! (*Shouting at ANTONIO.*) I won't let anybody rob me of my ideals even if I have been retired, d'you hear?!

ANTONIO: Get knotted, the lot of you! (*Off in a rage.*)

FIGARO: (*To PEDRILLO.*) You still have ideals, do you?

PEDRILLO: (*Seriously.*) Yes, I do.

(*Silence.*)

FANCHETTE: (*To FIGARO.*) If he hadn't had ideals then why would he have taken part in the Revolution?

FIGARO: To improve his position.

PEDRILLO: And that's not all. (*To FANCHETTE.*) Tell him.

FANCHETTE: We wanted to improve our position so that we'd become more decent human beings.

PEDRILLO: (*To FIGARO.*) Did you hear that, Mr Castle Warden?

FIGARO: Yes.

PEDRILLO: Just you remember that – (*He nods to him sadly and exits.*)

FIGARO: (*To FANCHETTE.*) Your husband is a fool.

FANCHETTE: (*Suddenly shouting at him.*) I'm not going to let you destroy everything that's human for me, not you!

FIGARO: You still haven't grasped the nub of the matter. We're living in times where the times themselves are more important than the people living in them. That's the sad fact.

Scene 3

It is one year later, once again abroad, in Cherubin's night-club, a small club and bar for émigrés. There is a bar, piano and separate booths. The entrance is backstage, to the right a door leads into the kitchen. It is evening but the club is still empty. SUSANNE is the waitress here and is just putting flowers and glasses on the tables. A CUSTOMER enters, he could be from Grosshadersdorf. Subdued lighting.

GUEST: (*Remaining standing.*) I appear to be your only customer.

SUSANNE: This is a night-club, sir, and we don't open until ten o'clock.

GUEST: So things only liven up later at your place?

SUSANNE: Yes, after midnight.

(*Silence.*)

GUEST: (*Looking at SUSANNE.*) Are you a princess?

SUSANNE: What? Me?

GUEST: In *émigré* clubs like this I hear that everyone is an aristocrat. The boss is a duke, the pianist's a baron and the waitress at least a member of the Royal Family –

(*He grins. CHERUBIN appears but unnoticed by SUSANNE and the GUEST; CHERUBIN is a plumpish, youthful gentleman with a rosy complexion masking its underlying brutality; he listens.*)

SUSANNE: (*Smiling.*) I'm not a princess.

GUEST: Well, what are you then?

SUSANNE: Nothing.

(*Silence.*)

GUEST: Pity, great pity. Well, perhaps I'll come back after midnight. Goodbye, lovely Miss Nothing! (*Exits.*)

SUSANNE: Goodbye, sir, goodbye!

CHERUBIN: (*Stepping forward.*) Susanne.

SUSANNE: (*Somewhat taken aback.*) Sir?

CHERUBIN: How often do I have to drum it into you that if somebody takes you for a princess, then do him a favour and just say yes, or at least give him an ambiguous smile; life's aim is not to rob good people of

their illusions and to bugger up our business – (*He
smiles.*) Talking of illusions: I cobbled together another
little song today, about a great love that is unrequited.
Could you think of a title?

SUSANNE: I can't write poetry, Herr von Cherubin.

CHERUBIN: What d'you think of the title 'Susanne'?

SUSANNE: (*Smiling.*) That's not a title.

CHERUBIN: Who knows? Perhaps it'll become an
international hit? – (*He sits down at the piano.*)

SUSANNE: With a title like 'Susanne' it certainly won't.

CHERUBIN: We'll see!

(*He plays and sings to a slow, kitschy tune.*)
Susanne I love you dear
Susanne I know quite clearly
With the Maytime urge
Towards you I surge –
Springtime is letting me know,
Susanne, my heart's had a blow.
My blood is yearning anew
It's crying within for you –
Susanne, my eyes grow dim
As I gaze upon heaven's rim
In death I'll be thanking you
For the torment you put me through – !
Well?

SUSANNE: Very tuneful.

CHERUBIN: Is that all you can say?

(*Silence.*)

SUSANNE: Herr von Cherubin, it hurts me to say this but
please don't name any more of your compositions after
me.

CHERUBIN: D'you know what you are?

SUSANNE: Yes, ungrateful.

CHERUBIN: You certainly are!

SUSANNE: Without your help I'd have starved.

CHERUBIN: You would indeed.

SUSANNE: I know.

(*Silence.*)

CHERUBIN: (*Fixing her with a friendly gaze.*) Incorrigible –

SUSANNE: I'll never marry again.

CHERUBIN: Was it that bad?

SUSANNE: Just leave me be, I'm a depraved creature – I show gratitude to people I despise and those I respect just seem a joke to me and that just about puts a stop to anything before it even starts.

CHERUBIN: It's a feeling that is not unfamiliar to me, but thanks to emigration I've managed to overcome it. I once used to be a great gigolo, but that's a few years ago now – (*He stops suddenly.*) Wait a minute, how long is it since we've been away from home?

SUSANNE: (*With a smile.*) Two hundred years.

CHERUBIN: (*Grinning.*) At the very least.

(*Silence.*)

SUSANNE: D'you know what date it is today? Today's the day he gets released.

CHERUBIN: Who does?

SUSANNE: The Count. It's exactly one year to the day that he was sentenced.

(*Silence.*)

CHERUBIN: Will he come here?

SUSANNE: I'm expecting him at any moment.

(*Silence.*)

CHERUBIN: If I ask you a question will you give me a straight answer?

SUSANNE: Gladly, if I can.

CHERUBIN: (*Slowly.*) Was there anything between you two, I mean you and the Count?

SUSANNE: Me and the Count? What on earth gave you that idea?

CHERUBIN: Well he certainly had the hots for you even before your marriage to Figaro –

SUSANNE: But you know perfectly well that nothing ever happened. Everyone knows that.

CHERUBIN: And now? Now that we're *émigrés*?

SUSANNE: Now more than ever can I say nothing's ever happened. Everything the Count ever did for me, even

when he got you to take me under your wing, he did out
of pure humanity.

CHERUBIN: That's a word you don't often hear.

SUSANNE: But that's how it was.

(*Silence.*)

CHERUBIN: Is it true that the Countess died of grief, grief
caused by the relationship between you and the Count?

SUSANNE: (*Yelling at him.*) Who says that? That is the
most despicable slander. Suggesting that the poor
Countess died because of me! You listen to me: I swear
to you by all that is holy to me that the poor Countess
died of influenza; and now may she walk through that
door, just as she was when she died, with her mouth
open, and curse me, if there was anything between me
and the Count; there was nothing, nothing, nothing. I
love another, one who has destroyed me and who
wouldn't let me become a mother and who I loathe like
the plague.

CHERUBIN: Figaro?

SUSANNE: Yes, the swine.

(*The lights go out gradually and the sound of CHERUBIN's
song 'Susanne' is heard, both sung and hummed by several
people and accompanied on the piano; when the lights come
up again the club is full of customers. A pianist is playing
and singing the song and the customers are humming the
tune, including the one who'd been in earlier; he has now
returned and is sitting at the bar.*)

SUSANNE: (*To CHERUBIN, who is standing behind the bar.*)
Has he had anything to eat?

CHERUBIN: He's still sitting in the kitchen.

CUSTOMER: (*To SUSANNE.*) Who's sitting in the kitchen?

SUSANNE: A passing acquaintance. (*She walks away and
goes on serving drinks.*)

CUSTOMER: (*Watching her go, he says to CHERUBIN.*)
Saucy little tart that one, isn't she?

CHERUBIN: (*Smiling.*) She's a princess. She doesn't like
admitting it because she's ashamed.

(*Silence.*)

CUSTOMER: (*Suddenly in a state of inebriation.*) Who the devil's sitting in the kitchen?

CHERUBIN: No one.

CUSTOMER: My good sir, don't you try and take the piss out of me!

CHERUBIN: Sir, the only people sitting in the kitchen are the staff and a beggar.

CUSTOMER: If it's a beggar then take him this brandy – (*He points at his large glass which is full.*) At once, d'you hear?

CHERUBIN: As you wish, sir. (*Exits angrily with the glass of brandy.*)

CUSTOMER: (*Calling out to SUSANNE.*) Hey, princess, who's that sitting out there in the kitchen? A prince? (*He grins.*)

SUSANNE: Yes. (*She turns her back on him.*)

INSPECTOR: (*Enters; to SUSANNE.*) Could I speak to the manager? Police.

SUSANNE: (*With a start.*) Of course! (*She hurries over to the kitchen door and calls out.*) Herr von Cherubin! (*CHERUBIN appears. SUSANNE points to the INSPECTOR.*) The gentleman would like to speak to you – (*Quietly.*) Police. (*She casts an anxious glance in the direction of the kitchen.*)

CHERUBIN: (*To the INSPECTOR.*) How can I help?

INSPECTOR: It's in relation to the following: you have in your employ a stateless waitress, whose work permit expired some four weeks ago –

SUSANNE: (*Interrupting him with relief.*) Oh, so it's only about me?

INSPECTOR: (*Sizing her up.*) Yes, only about you – (*He turns to CHERUBIN again.*) She must quit the job at once, otherwise she'll be in breach of the law and you, likewise, sir, and you'll lose your licence –

CHERUBIN: But I can't just put the poor girl out on the street –

INSPECTOR: (*Interrupting him.*) I'm sorry. Can't be helped! (*The COUNT appears at the kitchen door, the empty brandy-glass in his hand; he's a broken man, but still bears traces of*

*his former elegance; as he can't take alcohol any more he is
already completely befuddled by the one glass.*)
I'm only doing my duty and the individual unfortunately
doesn't count. The law's the law.

COUNT: (*Listening.*) Law?

CHERUBIN: (*To the COUNT.*) Please be quiet!

COUNT: I keep hearing the word 'law'.

INSPECTOR: (*To the COUNT.*) I'll ask you not to meddle
in official proceedings.

COUNT: I'm well acquainted with your official
proceedings and people damn well ought to meddle with
the laws – it's high time they did!

CUSTOMER: Bravo, prince!

INSPECTOR: (*To the COUNT.*) You keep your mouth shut!

COUNT: I most certainly won't keep my mouth shut, d'you
hear? Wouldn't dream of it!

CHERUBIN: (*To the INSPECTOR.*) The old man's been
drinking.

INSPECTOR: I hope he has, for his sake.

COUNT: (*Yelling at the INSPECTOR.*) You don't need to
have any hopes, for my sake. In fact I forbid you to! And
as far as drinking's concerned I only had one glass, but I
can still drink just as much as I used to, d'you hear, just
as much?! And now I'm going to give you my opinion –

INSPECTOR: We'll have none of your opinions expressed
here!

COUNT: Oh yes we shall –
(*He stops short, drops the glass and clutches at his heart and
begins to totter.*)

SUSANNE: Oh my God, Your Grace!

COUNT: (*Mumbling.*) I'll give everyone my opinion, even
the teacher –
(*He collapses on to a chair. SUSANNE goes to look after him.
The customers leave the bar.*)

INSPECTOR: (*To CHERUBIN.*) What's that? He's a
Count?

CHERUBIN: A certain Count Almaviva.
(*The INSPECTOR goes over to the COUNT and feels his
pulse.*)

SUSANNE: Is he dead?

INSPECTOR: Not a trace. Just alcohol – (*He takes out the COUNT's wallet, looks through his papers and suddenly stops short; quietly.*) Number eighty-seven. Released on –

CHERUBIN: Yes, yes, I know, it's a tragedy. He sold something that didn't belong to him –

INSPECTOR: Misappropriation?

CHERUBIN: Misappropriation and outright fraud – any child could have seen it coming, but not him. Yes, that's how it was, need versus negligence, the mitigating circumstances are outweighed by the aggravating ones.

COUNT: (*Coming round.*) Where's my hat?

CHERUBIN: In the kitchen.

SUSANNE: I'll get it – (*Exits to the kitchen.*)

INSPECTOR: (*To the COUNT.*) You can go. I was just looking to see who you were – (*He points to the wallet.*)

COUNT: (*Recognising his wallet.*) Ah, yes.
(*Silence.*)

INSPECTOR: (*Giving back the wallet.*) All in order.

COUNT: Have you seen the castle too?

INSPECTOR: (*Confused.*) What castle?

COUNT: My castle. Here you are – (*He pulls several photographs out of his wallet and shows them to the INSPECTOR.*) That was the park, it went up as far as the wood. And those, they're family pictures, memories, my wife and all the rest of it – (*He smiles.*)

INSPECTOR: If I were you I'd just go home now.

COUNT: Where to?

INSPECTOR: By the way, where do you live?

COUNT: D'you know the Esplanade Hotel? And the Carlton? I know 'em, know 'em all – It's been a pleasure, Inspector! Good night!

SUSANNE: (*Coming from the kitchen with the COUNT's hat and looking round in surprise.*) Where is he?

CHERUBIN: Gone.

SUSANNE: (*Anxiously.*) Without his hat?

INSPECTOR: Drunks never come to any harm.

CHERUBIN: One single glass –

INSPECTOR: He just can't take it any more.

CHERUBIN: Yes, that's right, a tragic case.

INSPECTOR: (*To SUSANNE.*) Come down the station in the morning, miss. Maybe the Good Lord'll arrange another few days' grace – Good night! (*Exits.*)

CHERUBIN: My respects, Inspector.

(*Silence.*)

SUSANNE: I'm not going to the police-station!

CHERUBIN: Are you mad?

SUSANNE: I couldn't give a damn about another few days' grace.

CHERUBIN: But what'll you live on if you don't have a work permit?

SUSANNE: I'll answer a letter.

CHERUBIN: What sort of a letter?

SUSANNE: A letter I've been carrying around with me for two weeks. I'd really like to know where he got the address from –

CHERUBIN: (*Listening attentively.*) Who?

SUSANNE: (*Ignoring the question.*) He wrote to ask if I'd go back to him. Said he was very lonely – (*She grins.*)

CHERUBIN: Who?

SUSANNE: Figaro.

(*Silence.*)

CHERUBIN: Where is he then?

SUSANNE: He's become castle warden and his conscience is pricking him.

(*Curtain.*)

Scene 4

Some years later and once more at the former country-seat of COUNT ALMAVIVA. FIGARO and all the orphans are sitting at a long table laid for lunch. They are eating. It is midday and FANCHETTE is bringing food; CARLOS, CAESAR and MAURIZIO are three orphans and they are thirteen, twelve and eight years old respectively; ELVIRA and ROSINE, orphans too, are both thirteen years old. The aged ANTONIO is squatting on a crate to one side and is fiddling around with an old-fashioned radio. He puts on the headphones, listening to music from a foreign radio station, occasionally conducting it to himself.

FIGARO: Fork on the left, knife on the right! (*To CARLOS.*)
Stop it, that roll belongs to Rosine! Don't be so greedy!
(*Pause.*)

ROSINE: Uncle Figaro, is it true that you used to be
married?

FIGARO: (*Confused.*) Me? Yes, I was.

ROSINE: (*To CARLOS.*) Told you so! I was right!

FIGARO: What d'you mean 'I told you so'? What's it got to
do with you whether I was married or not? (*Pause. To
ROSINE.*) How did you know anyway?

ROSINE: Auntie Fanchette told me.

FIGARO: (*To FANCHETTE.*) Well I never! My private life
is not a subject for general edification, please take good
note – (*To MAURIZIO.*) Don't eat with your fingers!
(*Pause. FIGARO listens carefully.*) Who's making that
disgusting slurping noise?

CARLOS: Me.

FIGARO: Kindly desist. A future leader must learn not to
slurp.

ELVIRA: Uncle Figaro, where is your wife now?

FIGARO: That's none of your business. Don't be so
impertinent!
(*ELVIRA starts crying.*)

FANCHETTE: (*Comforts her and says to FIGARO.*) The child
was only asking.

FIGARO: A child has no right to ask questions like that –
(*To MAURIZIO.*) Stop picking your nose!
(*Pause.*)

ELVIRA: (*Has now calmed down; spitefully.*) Is it true that
your wife was very wicked?

FIGARO: (*Confused.*) Wicked?

ELVIRA: Yes, 'cos Auntie Fanchette was arguing with Uncle
Pedrillo the other day and he said that she was just as
wicked as your wife –

FIGARO: (*To FANCHETTE.*) I would ask you not to row in
front of the children!

FANCHETTE: It's never me who starts.

ELVIRA: (*To FIGARO.*) And Uncle Pedrillo also said as well
that he was just as innocent as you are –

FIGARO: (*Interrupting her with severity.*) Well now. He ought
to know.

(*Pause.*)

ROSINE: Uncle Figaro, I don't believe it.

FIGARO: Don't believe what?

ROSINE: That you're innocent.

FIGARO: (*Confused.*) How's that? Why not?

ROSINE: (*Cheekily.*) 'Cos you don't look innocent.

FIGARO: What are you saying? How do I look? You take a
look at yourself, sweetie, before you look at me – What
cheek!

(*Pause.*)

CARLOS: Warden!

FIGARO: Well?

CARLOS: (*Mischievously hypocritical.*) I do believe it.

FIGARO: What d'you believe?

CARLOS: That you're both completely innocent –
(*He suddenly cannot control his laughter and all the other
children begin to laugh, pointing at FIGARO.*)

FIGARO: (*Looks round him for a moment not quite knowing
what to do, then his eye is caught by FANCHETTE who is
trying to suppress her laughter; she doesn't succeed and
FIGARO too cannot help laughing; to the children.*) Just you
wait! I'll show you who's the innocent party, you
miserable lot –

ANTONIO: (*Suddenly roaring at the children.*) Quiet!
(*Children all fall silent.*)

FIGARO: (*To ANTONIO.*) You shut up! (*To the children as he
stands up.*) Right, the meal's over! Up you get! Now say
grace!

CHILDREN: (*Standing up; in chorus.*) Death and destruction
to all our enemies!

ROSINE: (*Pointing to CAESAR.*) Uncle Figaro, he didn't say
grace, I heard him!

FIGARO: Heard him? Off you go, all of you! (*To CAESAR.*)
You stay right there!
(*Children exit with the exception of CAESAR. FANCHETTE
clears the table.*)

FIGARO: (*To CAESAR.*) Why didn't you join in the grace?

CAESAR: 'Cos I haven't got any enemies.

FIGARO: You think not?

CAESAR: I don't want to have any enemies.

(*Silence.*)

FIGARO: But if somebody hits you then you'd hit him back?

CAESAR: No.

FIGARO: And why not?

CAESAR: 'Cos nobody'd hit me if I didn't want them to.

FIGARO: (*Smiling.*) You're quite a philosopher –

CAESAR: What's a philosopher?

FIGARO: Philosophy's a forbidden subject.

(*Silence.*)

CAESAR: A few days ago somebody did hit me –

FIGARO: And what did you do?

CAESAR: I didn't hit him back.

FIGARO: (*Grinning.*) I suppose he was too big for you, was he?

CAESAR: No, he was too small for me.

(*Silence.*)

FIGARO: Come here. Closer than that. (*CAESAR obeys.*) What's your name?

CAESAR: Caesar.

(*Silence.*)

FIGARO: Are you new here?

CAESAR: No.

FIGARO: I wonder why I don't remember you –

CAESAR: We see one another every day.

(*Silence.*)

FIGARO: Hmm. Well, goodbye, young Caesar.

(*CAESAR exits.*)

ANTONIO: Figaro, I've just been listening to the news from abroad! What a prospect, we're on the way down!

FIGARO: The way down? (*He glances in the direction of CAESAR.*) On the contrary: on the way up!

ANTONIO: (*Perplexed.*) The way up?

FIGARO: Meeting that lad who won't hit back at somebody smaller than he is suddenly reminds me what the aim of the Revolution is – all about things that have recently been the target of my jokes and the subject of my more or less witty remarks which had no other effect than hurting or mocking others; all I succeeded in doing was alienating decent people – you see, if a Revolution had put me in an orphanage when I was young perhaps I'd have turned out differently –

ANTONIO: (*Maliciously.*) And what is your own personal aim?

FIGARO: I'm not telling.

ANTONIO: Big riddle, eh?

FIGARO: Yes, a riddle. What is it that's always looked for, never found and yet lost again and again –

(*ANTONIO shrugs his shoulders.*)

(*To FANCHETTE.*) Come here, I'll solve the riddle for you, but only for you, because you once asked me if I wasn't ashamed –

(*He smiles and whispers the answer in her ear, then gives her a friendly nod and exits.*)

ANTONIO: (*Watching him go in some surprise.*) What did he say?

FANCHETTE: I couldn't understand what he said.

ANTONIO: Always looked for, never found, and yet lost again and again – what is it?

FANCHETTE: What he said was, humanity.

Scene 5

In the depths of the forest near the border. SUSANNE and the COUNT are secretly crossing the border in order to return home. Only their voices can be heard as it is a pitch-black night.

COUNT: Where are you?

SUSANNE: Over here.

COUNT: I can't see a thing.

SUSANNE: This is the blackest night of my life –

(*She lets out a scream.*)

COUNT: What's the matter?

SUSANNE: I just stepped in something soft.

(A pale moon breaks through the clouds and now the returning fugitives become visible.)

COUNT: The moon is waxing – just like the last time. Then I was leaving the land of my fathers so as not to be murdered; now I'm returning home, through the very same forest, so as not to be locked up again. Ah well, Needs Must When the Devil Drives – *(He smiles.)* Today I don't bother to ask myself what crime I committed that made it necessary for me to sneak over the border in secret –

SUSANNE: But Your Grace, you haven't committed any crime!

COUNT: Haven't I? I miscalculated. 'In two months it'll all be over' – *(He grins.)* Figaro was right. *(Looking round.)* Are we over the border yet?

SUSANNE: I remember every clearing here. To the right the lake, to the left the gorge. It's all behind us now.

COUNT: What do you actually hope to get out of taking me with you?

SUSANNE: *(Confused.)* What d'you mean?

COUNT: You don't exactly imagine they'll be delighted when I turn up at home?

SUSANNE: But your Grace, we've already discussed all that! We're going to go to Figaro secretly and find out how the land lies –

COUNT: *(Interrupting her.)* Did you actually write and tell him we were coming?

SUSANNE: No, he doesn't know anything about it yet. I wanted to but I couldn't, I just tore the letter up every time. I must talk to him in person.
(Silence.)

COUNT: He's become castle warden, hasn't he?

SUSANNE: Your Grace *knows* that!

COUNT: And what's become of me?
(He grins.)

SUSANNE: Your Grace, I can see a light!

COUNT: *(Without looking up.)* I can't see anything.

SUSANNE: Come on now –

COUNT: (*Interrupting her.*) No. That fallen tree over there
looks like a bed to me. Yes, the bed was on the left, the
sofa on the right. She used to sleep on the sofa, it was too
short for me – (*Looking heavenwards.*) D'you sleep more
comfortably now?
(*Silence.*)

SUSANNE: (*Looking heavenwards.*) It's raining.
(*Now the wind begins to get up, slowly at first.*)

COUNT: You go, Susanne, he asked you to, nobody's
asking me to do anything. I'm staying.

SUSANNE: Here?

COUNT: It was never really clear to me why I followed
you back; only now am I beginning to see that what I
wanted was to sleep in my own bed – yes, you see, the
sofa was too short for me –

SUSANNE: (*Tearfully.*) But, Your Grace, please don't
confuse the situation still further! What d'you want to
stay here in the wood for?

COUNT: (*Pointing at the tree-trunk.*) There's my bed.
(*A strong gust of wind blows. The moon disappears behind
the clouds, the night is once again pitch-black. All that can be
heard is SUSANNE's voice sounding further and further
away, as it becomes drowned out by the storm.*)

SUSANNE: Your Grace! Where on earth are you? Please
answer me! Your Grace! Your Grace!
(*Silence.*

*The moon once more breaks through the clouds and we see the
COUNT alone.*)

COUNT: (*Removing his coat and testing the belt for strength; as
he does so he hums Cherubin's song 'Susanne'; suddenly he says
to himself.*) My wife always used to say we're at school
and waiting for the summer holidays to begin – (*He gazes
heavenwards.*) Is there long to wait, Sir?

VOICE: Stay where you are.
(*The COUNT starts with fright and listens.*)
Where are you going?
(*The COUNT stares into the wood and says nothing.*)

SERGEANT: (*Whose voice it was, steps forward.*) Papers?

155

COUNT: (*With a strange smile.*) What?

SERGEANT: Your papers. Passport, that sort of thing.

COUNT: (*Grinning.*) What's that?

SERGEANT: Don't you try to be funny! Who are you anyway?

COUNT: Me?

SERGEANT: (*Impatiently.*) Who else d'you think?

COUNT: (*Slowly.*) I am 'His Grace the Count' Almaviva –

SERGEANT: Almaviva?!

COUNT: (*Smiling.*) Yes, that is correct.

(*SERGEANT stares at him in amazement; he swiftly pulls himself together and blows his police whistle. The GUARD appears.*)

INSPECTOR: (*To the COUNT.*) In the name of the people, I arrest you!

(*Curtain.*)

Scene 6

Once more at the former country seat of COUNT ALMAVIVA. FANCHETTE is sitting by the gate mending her husband's trousers. It is a warm autumn morning. FANCHETTE is singing Cherubin's song to herself.

FANCHETTE: Springtime is letting me know,
Susanne, my heart's had a blow.
My blood is yearning anew,
It's crying within for you.
(*FIGARO appears in the doorway, stops and listens.
FANCHETTE does not notice him and goes on singing.*)
Susanne I love you dearly
Susanne I know quite clearly
With the Maytime urge
Towards you I surge –
(*Only now does she notice FIGARO; abruptly she stops singing.*)

FIGARO: What's that Susanne song you're singing?

FANCHETTE: Don't you know it? It's the latest hit, took the world by storm in just a few days.

FIGARO: Really? Seems to me that pop songs are more infectious than revolutionary verse. Has the post come yet?

FANCHETTE: Yes. Here it is – (*Handing him several letters.*)

FIGARO: (*Looking at the letters.*) Is that all?

FANCHETTE: (*Fixing him with her gaze.*) What are you actually waiting for?

FIGARO: A letter. A private affair.

FANCHETTE: (*Mildly ironic as she spreads her husband's trousers out.*) You and private affairs don't seem to go together at all, you just live for the castle and the kids –

FIGARO: (*Interrupting her.*) Tell me, d'you think the kids like me?

FANCHETTE: What daft questions you do ask! You're Top God Almighty for those kids, they'd steal and rob and murder for you –

FIGARO: (*Smiling.*) D'you think so? (*He looks round.*) When's the next post due?

FANCHETTE: There's no delivery tomorrow.

FIGARO: Hmm –

(*He is about to go off into the castle.*)

SERGEANT: (*Enters hurriedly right and salutes.*) Good morning, Warden.

FIGARO: Good morning to you, Sergeant. Everything in order?

SERGEANT: Beg to report, sir, an important arrest. A man. He'd smuggled his way over the border and we came across him not far from the gorge. Claims he's Count Almaviva –

FIGARO: (*Interrupting.*) What?!

FANCHETTE: Almaviva? Good God!

FIGARO: Where is he?

SERGEANT: We've locked him up in the cellar.

FIGARO: Let's go! Come along, Sergeant! (*Exits swiftly left with the SERGEANT.*)

PEDRILLO: (*Entering left in a state of excitement.*) Hey, Fanchette, guess who's back? Count Almaviva, His Honour the monster! Well, I'll have a word or two to say to that cynical old sod who raped my wife –

FANCHETTE: (*Interrupting him.*) Come off it, you fool! Can't you leave politics alone for once!

PEDRILLO: Rape is not a matter of politics, I'll have you know!

(*Silence.*)

FANCHETTE: (*Slowly.*) Pedrillo, there's something I've got to tell you but please, don't despise me for it –

PEDRILLO: I don't despise even the lowest of the low. What's up?

FANCHETTE: I'm frightened. If you dredge up all that business about what the Count did to me there'll only be trouble –

PEDRILLO: Justice must be seen to be done, and no one goes around committing rape and gets away with it, not around here they don't! We haven't sunk that low yet.

FANCHETTE: Pedrillo, I told you a lie.

PEDRILLO: (*Stopping short.*) What are you trying to tell me?

FANCHETTE: (*Slowly.*) What I'm trying to tell you is that it wasn't a proper rape –

PEDRILLO: Not a proper rape?! Well what *was* it?

FANCHETTE: (*Smiling uneasily.*) It just wasn't.

(*Silence.*)

PEDRILLO: (*Fixing his eyes on her.*) So it was just a proper little lie, was it?

FANCHETTE: Please don't be angry with me, please –

PEDRILLO: Perhaps I'm supposed to be *glad* that he didn't rape you?! The bottom suddenly falls out of my world, great mountains of theories go tumbling down with every concept of what is right and what is wrong. I've always said the same thing: the only place left is the pub.

(*Silence.*)

FANCHETTE: What are you going to do now?

PEDRILLO: I'm certainly not going to hang myself!

FANCHETTE: (*Slowly.*) D'you want a divorce?

PEDRILLO: (*Yelling at her.*) Are you trying to make even more trouble for me? There can be no question of divorce, because of the children for a start; but let's get

one thing quite clear right away: after this confession of
yours you have absolutely no right to prescribe when I
go to the pub, nor how long I choose to remain there,
d'you understand?!
(*He leaves her standing there and exits left.*)

FANCHETTE: (*Alone; watching him go.*) You don't love me
any more – (*Exits into the castle.*)

FIGARO: (*Entering right together with the SERGEANT and
followed by two children, CARLOS and MAURIZIO; to the
SERGEANT.*) I stand by what I said! I take full
responsibility!

SERGEANT: Please, Warden, please –

FIGARO: (*Interrupting him.*) There's no 'please' about it! An
order's an order and that's that!

SERGEANT: Very good, Warden, sir.
(*He salutes and exits left. FIGARO is about to go into the
castle.*)

CARLOS: Warden!

FIGARO: (*Stopping.*) What's the matter?

CARLOS: Count Almaviva should be shot immediately,
shouldn't he?

FIGARO: Who says so?

CARLOS: I do.

FIGARO: (*Giving him a serious look.*) You do, do you?

CARLOS: Yes, because he's a political criminal.

MAURIZIO: (*To CARLOS.*) No he thouldn't be thot, he ·
thould he thwown in pwithon for life!

FIGARO: (*Severely.*) And why should he be imprisoned?

MAURIZIO: Becoth pwithon for life ith a worthe
punithment, teacher thaid.

FIGARO: Did he now? (*Aside.*) I can see I shall have to give
this teacher some lessons in humour – (*To the children.*)
Now listen to me, you two officers of the law! Firstly, I'd
rather you go and smash a few windows in than dabble
in politics! Secondly: Count Almaviva is not a criminal –

CARLOS: (*Interrupting him.*) But he's a Count!

FIGARO: Were you ever a Count?

CARLOS: (*Baffled.*) No.

FIGARO: There you are then! Don't talk about things you know nothing about. You listen to me, if you should meet Count Almaviva then you greet him respectfully, be polite and well-behaved, because he is an old man and you are snotty little kids, and if he has committed any crimes then he certainly won't be waiting for you to pass sentence. And anyway: why d'you want to shoot a man and lock him up for life without so much as a by-your-leave? What's he done to you, or to you? Aren't you both ashamed of yourselves? Be careful, perhaps when you get old they'll be saying every orphan's a criminal and there'll only be counts left and the counts'll lock up all the orphans and shoot them – so there, and now go and smash a few windows in, off you go!
(*The children go off in silence. SUSANNE comes on left. FIGARO catches sight of her.*)
Susanne!
(*He stares at her. SUSANNE looks at him but says nothing. He passes his hand over his eyes in some confusion.*)
Why didn't you answer my letter?

SUSANNE: (*Unable to conceal her smile.*) Should I have written?

FIGARO: What am I saying? It just hasn't sunk in yet that you're here in front of me – I've been waiting for a letter for weeks –

SUSANNE: Figaro, I hear you've arrested the Count?

FIGARO: Which count?

SUSANNE: Count Almaviva!

FIGARO: Oh yes, him. Forgive me, I'm still rather confused –

SUSANNE: (*Cutting in.*) Just you see to it nothing happens to the Count, d'you hear me? It's my fault that he came back, and it'd be terrible if you lot did him any harm, over there he always helped me so much –

FIGARO: (*Interrupting her.*) Why d'you keep going on about the Count when we haven't seen one another for so long?

SUSANNE: Because that is more important to me at the moment!

FIGARO: (*Pricking up his ears.*) More important?

SUSANNE: Please promise me that nothing will happen to him!

FIGARO: You really believe I'd let anything happen to the Count?

SUSANNE: I don't know.

FIGARO: You don't know? Just you wait a minute! Of course the Count can't be saved and if he were pardoned then he'd be jailed for life –

SUSANNE: What?! Figaro, you must save him!

FIGARO: I can't do that. Right is right.

SUSANNE: There are two kinds of right –

FIGARO: (*Interrupting her.*) Since when?

SUSANNE: Since when? You're asking me? Those were always your theories – oh, now I begin to see how much you lied to me in your letter, all that about humanity, but with you it's nothing but words!

FIGARO: No. You've come back yet you still believe me capable of every kind of wickedness and for that reason you deserve to be disappointed.

SUSANNE: You haven't changed.

FIGARO: I think I have.

(*Silence.*)

SUSANNE: I came back to you because my work permit was taken away.

FIGARO: Glad to hear it.

SUSANNE: It's only because I couldn't get anything to eat over there that I came back here to you.

FIGARO: Don't believe you.

SUSANNE: It's true.

FIGARO: No, it's not.

SUSANNE: Why should I lie to you?

FIGARO: Why do you lie to yourself? Does it make you feel good? Makes no odds to me.

(*Silence.*)

SUSANNE: Conscience prick you, did it? (*She grins.*)

FIGARO: If you ask me like that I'll say no.

SUSANNE: Why did you ask me to come?

FIGARO: Because I need you.

SUSANNE: (*Scornfully.*) What for?

FIGARO: Please don't ask such a stupid question! (*Silence. He slowly walks over to her and stops right in front of her.*) Susanne. You once asked me what it'd be like when we're old and there isn't anyone there to call our own? Our whole lives will have been pointless –

SUSANNE: (*Staring at him wide-eyed.*) And you said, it didn't have much point anyway – and I said, then I'd rather die straight away –

FIGARO: And I said I was very fond of you. D'you remember?

SUSANNE: (*Softly.*) Yes, but I said that wasn't enough on its own –

FIGARO: That's right. (*He nods to her with a smile.*) But today, today I'm no longer afraid of the future – (*Nearby the sound of a window being smashed. They both listen. Another crash of glass.*)

ANTONIO: (*Comes running on from the left.*) Figaro, those little bastards are smashing the windows in, I'll pull their ears off for them!

FIGARO: You'll control yourself! I've given them permission to smash the windows.

ANTONIO: Permission? (*Another crash of glass.*)

FIGARO: I promised them they'd be allowed to, provided they don't dabble in politics.

ANTONIO: That's going too far. (*Another crash.*)

FIGARO: Now that really has gone too far! (*To ANTONIO.*) Well? (*He points to SUSANNE.*) And what do you think of my wife?

ANTONIO: We've already said hello. (*The COUNT appears in the doorway; he looks well-groomed but very tired.*) Good God, His Grace Count Almaviva!

COUNT: (*Smiling.*) Ah, my dear old Antonio – you still alive too?

ANTONIO: Not for long, noble Count, not for long!

COUNT: That's true for all of us. (*Suddenly he stares to the left.*) Hey, my big pine is missing over there –

162

ANTONIO: The lightning got it –

COUNT: I'm relieved to hear it. I thought perhaps you'd had it cut down – (*He smiles and looks round.*) – Yes the benches are still there under the trees and the trees haven't left their places and the meadows have stayed at home – Figaro!

FIGARO: (*Walking over to him.*) Yes, Your Grace?

COUNT: Am I really free now?

FIGARO: Definitely, Your Grace.

COUNT: And I am to sleep in my old room?

FIGARO: Definitely, Your Grace.

COUNT: Is the Revolution over then?

FIGARO: On the contrary, Your Grace. It is only now that the Revolution has been victorious, now that it is no longer necessary to lock people up in cellars, people who can't help being its enemies.

SUSANNE: Figaro!

(*She runs over to him and embraces him.*
And once again the sound of crashing glass is heard.)

The End.